THE DEFINITIVE GUIDE TO GHOSTWRITING

THE DEFINITIVE GUIDE TO GHOSTWRITING

ALEE ANDERSON & ALICE SULLIVAN

GATSBY HOUSE PUBLISHING

ISBN: 979-8-9930129-1-9 (ebook)
ISBN: 979-8-9930129-0-2 (paperback)

Published in association with Gatsby House
gatsbyhousebooks.com

Acknowledgements

To Mary and Michael and especially Mom (Mama Llama).
Thank you for always believing in me. I love you.

—Alice

For Donna, whose unwavering belief
in me taught me to believe in others.

—Alee

Table of Contents

Yes, You Can Make a Great Living as a Ghostwriter

We see you there, Writer, thinking about writing. Wondering if there will come a day you might shed your corporate, 9-to-5 existence and write full-time. You imagine yourself sitting at a computer with a mug of coffee or tea (read: possibly wine) in your hand, comfy slippers on your feet, and Microsoft Word open. You're trying to figure out how writing could serve you as both a creative outlet and a financial inlet.

Mind if we interrupt your contemplation? We've got some answers to your wonderings, and they are, in order: Yes and YES. Yes, if that is your dream, you can ditch your 9-to-5 (responsibly, of course). And YES, not only can you make a living writing, but it can also be the basis of a thriving business. (And contrary to popular belief, you do not need to memorize all the comma rules.)

How do we know? Well, we—Alice Sullivan and Alee Anderson—are both professional ghostwriters who have built multiple six-figure freelance writing businesses, and we want to empower you, writer friend, to do the same. Honest. This is neither a trick nor one of those seminars promising to jumpstart your freelance business without helping you at all. This is a guide—a handbook, even—specifically designed to help you build and grow your freelance ghostwriting business from beginning to booming. While we both focus on nonfiction books, you can ghostwrite any content that you desire—from fiction novels to TED Talks, speeches, web copy, music lyrics, technical works, and more.

Just seven years into ghostwriting, Alee's annual earnings have grown from $38,000/year to multiple six figures. Her husband was able to leave traditional work and stay home to pursue his own art. Alice is currently in her tenth consecutive six-figure year and has been able to invest in real estate with her extra income, with plans to continue buying more properties. This is what we want for you. We want you to have options!

We firmly believe the creative space should be a community of collaboration. After years of mentoring and being mentored—Alice is even Alee's friend-turned-mentor-turned-collaborator—we decided the best way to honor our philosophy is to share the wealth of knowledge we've gained from both the publishing industry and the world of building freelance businesses from scratch.

Throughout this book, we'll take you through our "Holy-shit-did-I-just-end-my-career?" and "Do-I-have-enough-money-for-a-single-taco?" moments, give you a transparent look into our individual journeys to financial independence, and dish on all the reasons freelancers are entitled to—and can earn—all the same benefits salaried employees enjoy. We can take vacation time, contribute to retirement plans, buy health insurance, invest in different opportunities, and live whatever lifestyles we've dreamed of.

Although self-employment has traditionally been seen as the "lesser" desired employment status, the truth is, when you're free from salaried work, you remove the ceiling on your earning potential. Together, we've learned that the sky really is the limit.

You'll hear from us together and separately. More than anything, though, this journey is about you and what you are willing to put into it (be prepared to be an active participant!). But if you haven't figured it out yet, we're already your biggest cheerleaders.

CHAPTER 1

Is the Freelance Life Right for You?

We'll be the first to acknowledge that a lot has changed in the professional landscape. Seemingly overnight, we went from a world where the professional workforce was largely confined to the three walls of a cubicle to one where many people can enjoy working from home. Yet, for most, working a corporate job from home still feels confining. Yes, you can pet the dog while you work and enjoy snacks from your own fridge, but in this scenario, your time is hardly your own. Many traditionally employed folks have their productivity monitored to an insane degree, having to limit bathroom breaks so they can wiggle their mouse to prove they are online during work hours. Ultimately, some may find it easier to return to the office than navigate the politics and complexities of working from home.

In all this, many have looked to freelancing as a viable solution, but this comes with a healthy dose of fear. People wonder whether there will be enough work to go around, if they'll make enough money to survive, and whether they'll be able to make it all work. We writers have the added fears that our skill set isn't one that people care to pay for, or that we'll be replaced by AI—that it's just a passion of ours and not a viable way to make a living. We're here to tell you that, although your fears are valid, they are largely unfounded. You can have a thriving career as a freelance writer. The only question is whether the freelance life is right for you.

WHAT DOES IT MEAN TO BE A FREELANCER?

Let's start with the very basics—a freelancer (or a contractor) is someone who works on their own (as opposed to part of an established company) to complete assignments for a set fee. Typically, this is short-term work, but it can also extend to longer-term projects that might span months or even years (since some projects go over 12 months) depending on the scope of each assignment you tackle.

WHAT DOES IT MEAN TO BE A FREELANCE WRITER?

Freelance writers perform a myriad of services from journalism to screenwriting, copywriting to short-form content creation, and what we do best—ghostwriting books. Being a freelance writer is a rollercoaster of creativity and hustle. It is freedom mingled with heavy responsibility. You dance between deadlines and inspiration, juggling multiple projects at a time. Sometimes it's fun and sometimes it's overwhelming, but it's also incredibly fulfilling. The flexibility to work from anywhere is liberating, but it demands discipline. You're both CEO and employee, managing finances, marketing, and client relations. Though writing is traditionally solitary, freelancing allows you to engage with clients regularly and make close contact with other writers in your field. There's no limit on your earning potential as a freelancer. With steady work and discipline, you can easily begin earning a lucrative income within your first five years.

WHAT EXACTLY IS FREELANCE LIFE LIKE?

Like any lifestyle, there are pros and cons to freelance life, and some people will enjoy it more than others. Some will thrive from day one and love the autonomy, while others will slowly gain steam over time, widening their circle and building a solid portfolio of work. Some writers will decide that freelancing part-time, in addition to a primary job, is right for them. Others may try freelancing for a while and then choose to return to a salaried position. All of these choices are perfectly okay. After all, you need to do what's best for you.

One thing we can say, though, is that no day is the same for a freelancer. For instance, a week in your life could easily look like this:

Monday	Work for 10 hours on a rush project. Go to bed exhausted but feeling accomplished.
Tuesday	Answer 30 emails, read three chapters of a book for research, then spend the rest of the day at the spa.
Wednesday	Read and research for two hours, meet friends for lunch, write for two hours.
Thursday	Write from 5 a.m. to 10 a.m., break for lunch and emails, then take a long walk at your favorite park before working another 90 minutes to wrap up the day.
Friday	Client meetings in the morning, administrative tasks in the afternoon. Plan out the next week's calendar.
Saturday and Sunday	Relax! On Friday or Sunday afternoon, it is smart to review the upcoming week's schedule for a few minutes so you can start work on Monday feeling prepared.

Some weeks, depending on your projects, you may only work 20 hours. Other weeks, you might work 50-60 hours, including weekends, if a deadline is near (although we've worked hard to minimize those longer weeks so we can have weekends off). Early in your freelance career, it might be the norm to work seven days a week. But our hope is that you can set a boundary to take the weekend (or whatever days work for you) off from the very start! You need time to recharge.

The beauty of freelancing is that you're in charge of your schedule. Some colleagues structure most of their days from 9 a.m. to 5 p.m. because they thrive on routine and structure. Others like to get up early (or late) to work around other commitments. They can do that because it works for them—and that's the whole point: as a freelancer, the world is your oyster.

CHALLENGES OF FREELANCE LIFE: SCHEDULING AND UNPREDICTABLE EARNINGS

Nothing is without its challenges. While the benefits of freelance life include wonderful things like flexible scheduling, constant opportunities to hone your writing skills and build your community, and the ability to choose your own clients and set your own rates, challenges do pop up. And since you are the one in charge, you are also the one who must overcome these challenges.

One of the questions you'll need to reflect on and dig deep about is whether you are okay with a level of unpredictability, particularly with your earnings. Some months will be high-earning and others will be low, depending on your project load and payment arrangements. That's just how it is sometimes. Remember to save as much as you're able to, so that when those low-income months arrive, you won't be as anxious.

(Alice) Maximizing Self-Care in the Slow Seasons

Recently, I had two projects that ended at the same time—one because it wasn't a good fit, and the client and I decided to end our working relationship midway through the project, and the other because the work flowed so easily that we finished the project a month early.

I had some anxiety about the financial implications of losing several months of payments that I'd already accounted for in my yearly budget from the canceled job. But the overwhelming truth is those months ended up being some of the best months I've had in a long time for self-care and fun, because I had so much free time to do whatever I wanted. I took a watercolor painting class with my mom and sister, signed up for ceramics, tried glass paperweight-making, gardened a lot, and started playing volleyball again.

Not being obligated to 40-60 hours of work each week freed up time to do more of the things I enjoy as I conversed and negotiated with new potential clients. And it wasn't the end of the world financially, because I had several months' worth of savings set aside.

For me, that experience provided a healthy perspective shift. Even when I have less work, I don't have to sit around on my butt unless that is really what I love to do. Instead, I can do all the things I wish I had time for when my schedule is busy. So, take the classes. Do the hobbies. Read the books. And learn to work with the lulls in business instead of against them.

(Alee) Rescheduling to Prioritize Wellness and Healing

Earlier this week, I woke up with a bad cold. My brain was foggy, but I forced myself to sit down at my desk and work anyway. Looking back, I see that I didn't have to punish my body in that way—and, if I'm honest, the work I actually managed to produce was total trash. My schedule would have easily allowed me to push those tasks to the next day, and I would have felt better while working, which means the quality of my work would have been far better. It's important to remember that flexibility is one of the many gifts of freelance life, and we should always take advantage of it!

SCHEDULING YOUR DAYS AND YOUR WEEKS

Managing your schedule as a freelancer can be an ongoing challenge. The number of meetings will ebb and flow, in cycles, depending on the projects you accept. The key is to establish a pattern during the week and try to stick to it.

For example, you could set aside Mondays for administrative tasks and use the rest of the week for meetings and writing work. You might also prefer to take off Fridays at noon, allowing you to slide into the weekend a little early.

One week, you may have very few meetings. The following week, you might have so many meetings that you end up ordering lunch three days in a row. While it can be tempting to load up on meetings—after all, it's a good sign that so many people want to speak with you—it can drain your energy and leave you with little to no writing time if you're not careful. And if you're an introvert like Alice, too many meetings can make you want to hide in a cave. (For reference, the most meetings Alice has scheduled in one week is 28. Don't do that. For an introvert, that's a lot of interaction—too much to get any writing done!)

But why so many meetings? Because while you're working on current projects, ideally, you're also fielding calls for the next batch. Each month, you'll likely receive new leads for work, and while most of those can be handled by email, some will naturally lead to phone or video calls.

This is where you can be intentional about the language you use. Instead of leaving your entire schedule open to the client and asking, "When are you available?" try asking, "Are you available on Tuesday at either 9:00 or 11:00?" Select a couple of days during the week and create time blocks of availability, then offer those times to the client. This way, they have options, but you are still in charge of your schedule. You might also consider using a scheduling tool like Calendly, where you predetermine your available days and times, and then let potential clients book a call using your link.

Remember to always prioritize your own needs first, including blocking out holidays and weekends! We can't tell you how many times we've forgotten federal holidays, our own birthdays, or other important dates. If you don't prioritize your needs—doctor's appointments, vacations, concerts, gym time, hobbies, date nights, etc.—they won't happen, and you'll soon feel overwhelmed.

As a freelancer, you have to be willing to advocate for yourself, figuring out what works for you and what doesn't. While this book is meant to help you plan for a freelance ghostwriting career, you also need to ask yourself: How will I plan for slower months? How do I manage conflict? What boundaries can I set for myself? What does regular self-care look like for me? And how will I ensure my connections stay consistent and social needs are met?

This last question about maintaining connection is, perhaps, the one you should spend some extra time considering as you begin this journey. If you're an extrovert who already has a solid weekly routine and great social calendar, good for you!

If you're an introvert who can't even work in coffee shops because of the noise and distractions, you might need to put more effort into getting out of the house. And you'll want to be mindful of the times you decide to be super social but end up scheduling so many events that you feel depleted. It's a fine line, but you'll figure it all out as you go.

FIND YOUR COMMUNITY

Ultimately, Dear Writer, one of the most important questions to ask yourself as you forge your own freelance ghostwriting path is: Am I surrounding myself with people who lift me up? We can't overstate the benefits of leaning into your community of creatives and having the right people in your corner.

Yes, there is a lot of competition and ego in the writing profession. However, within ghostwriting, we have found a wonderfully supportive and generous community. Unlike some other areas of publishing, most ghostwriters understand that there is plenty of work to go around. They're usually willing to help one another, share advice, and refer work if they are too busy to take on a project.

You can start finding your community by joining Facebook groups, LinkedIn networks and local writing meetups, and by attending industry conferences and networking events.

As you begin your journey, seek out people who are committed to the ideas of mentorship and friendship, kindness and encouragement. Keep close those who want to help other artistic people develop their skills. These relationships aren't just nice to have; they're the ones that will keep you sane when you inevitably feel like you've hit a wall.

START WHERE YOU ARE, BUT DEFINITELY START

Let's circle back to the big question: Is the freelance writer life right for you? To answer that, consider these questions: Are you the go-to words person for people in your life? Do others ask you to write and edit resumes, emails, letters, and papers because you just "get" how to say things? How would you feel if you could create an income with this skill set?

We are led to believe that "feast or famine" is all we can expect in creative professions. The struggling writer/editor/actor/creator is a trope we all know too well. Even when we're young, we're warned by well-meaning people that our dreams are only side-hustle-worthy, so we should make sure we also get a "real job." However, if your answers to those earlier questions are "YES," and you are a driven, determined professional, you may have just discovered your calling.

Of course, we understand that it's unlikely you can drop everything and write full-time starting tomorrow. But what you can do is create a plan, start building connections, and begin where you are. It's important to understand where you're starting, but it's just as important to have a clear picture of where you want to go. Throughout this guide, you'll find practical exercises and tools to help you take action as you envision and lay the foundation of the life you deserve (a life that is totally attainable, by the way). Remember, every small step you take now leads you closer to the life you've been dreaming of.

OUR TYPICAL WORKDAYS

Alice:

Most mornings, I get up at 5:30 or 6:00 a.m., and after feeding Bailey (my cat), I'm at my desk by 6:30 a.m. I sometimes wake up in the morning with mild anxiety about the work to be done that day and the week ahead. So, I try to wait until that anxious buzzing has subsided before I start working. When possible, I like to start the day with a sense of control over my emotions, schedule, and projects.

Routine and organization at the start of the day really help me. I have always used a day planner, but I also keep a separate list on a notepad of all the things I want to accomplish, including people I need to call and even reminders for groceries. It works for me. There is so much gratification in scratching items off my to-do list. It helps me feel accomplished and gives me a boost of confidence.

One of the very first things I do every day, without fail, is to make my bed—not hotel-perfect by any means, but I always pull the sheets up and put the pillows back in place. That one tiny action helps me start the day right.

Alee:

I wake up and go through the insanity of getting all three of my kiddos to school. Once everyone is dropped off, I have a cup of coffee, then work out for an hour and hit the sauna at the YMCA if I can. Once I've taken care of myself, I come into my office with my overflowing purse, some snacks, and my dog by my side. The first thing I do is put on my hyperfixation song of the week while I get the room ready. I gather my fluffy pillow, heating pad, and blanket. Then, I light incense, all my candles, and palo santo.

I tend to start the day anxious, so my first move is always to look at my to-do list and check in with my assistant to make sure I know who is doing what. I write a fresh to-do list on paper, in order of urgency. I break down my list by client. Sometimes, I even break down my list by word count. I will literally write "1,000 words" four times if I need to write 4,000 words, just to get the dopamine hit of crossing off one item at a time. Then, I set a one-hour timer to respond to emails and complete my "get ready" and administrative tasks. Then, I start my day, officially.

TAKE ACTION

Create a Vision Board:
What Do You Want Your Life to Look Like?

Whether you are fresh out of college, a transitioning professional, or looking to diversify your income, it's essential to create a vision for what you want your life to look like. Your first assignment is to create a vision board using the following prompts:

- What are your personal and professional priorities?

- How do you want to *feel* as you work in this profession?

- What do you want your writing life to look like?

- What does success look like or feel like to you?

If you're a tactile learner, grab some poster board, scissors, and magazines. If you're the digital type, open a new file with your favorite brainstorming program (Miro is great for this). Don't be afraid to get real. Be transparent with yourself and dig deep.

This marks the beginning of building a new life and career, giving you the space and freedom to map out your dreams and goals. Keep it somewhere you'll see regularly, and yet the vision board serve as a reminder of what you're working toward. As you learn and experience more, allow it to change and evolve with you.

CHAPTER 2

What Is Ghostwriting Exactly?

Ghostwriting is the art of writing on behalf of someone else without receiving public credit for the work. It's like being a literary shadow. From books to articles, speeches to blog posts, ghostwriters lend their skills to individuals, businesses, and even celebrities who seek polished and professional content under their name. In the best working relationships, the ghostwriter's voice seamlessly blends with the client's, crafting prose that reflects their ideas, experiences, and expertise.

This type of collaboration requires a deep understanding of the client's vision, voice, and audience. We assess this by conducting extensive interviews and performing research to capture the essence of their message. Our writing is carefully tailored to match each client's preferences, with the goal of creating content that is well-structured, compelling, and informative.

While the ghostwriter remains largely invisible, our personal touch significantly shapes the final product. Despite the absence of public acclaim, ghostwriting offers a unique blend of challenges and rewards. It demands versatility, as we must navigate diverse topics and be able to match a wide range of voices. Financially, ghostwriting can be incredibly lucrative, especially for those who excel at capturing their clients' voices and visions. These are just some of the reasons we love what we do.

So why would someone hire a ghostwriter? Is it because they're lazy or uninspired? Nope, that's far from the truth. It's for people who have a great story to tell but don't have the time, interest, or ability to physically write it themselves.

Some clients we worked with needed writing assistance because they were running several businesses and had busy family lives that left them with very little free time. We've also worked with people who may not be were not necessarily able to write, in the traditional sense. Many authors who are fantastic verbal storytellers struggle with ADD, ADHD, dyslexia, or have other limitations that prohibit them from physically writing, speaking, or typing. Others seek assistance because English isn't their first language.

It doesn't make their story any less valid or impactful that they didn't physically sit and write each word themselves. Instead, the ghostwriting partnership is a testament to how passionate these clients are; despite their circumstances, they are determined to find writers who can help them bring their stories to life.

WHAT CAN BE GHOSTWRITTEN?

You can be a ghostwriter for all kinds of written material, not just books. Articles, web copy, speeches, promotional materials, courses—essentially, if words are involved, it can be ghostwritten.

Here's a helpful list of items:

Types of Ghostwriting

- Books (fiction and nonfiction)
- Book proposals and query letters
- Ebooks and pamphlets
- Workbooks and study guides
- Online course material

- Song lyrics
- Website content
- Magazine articles
- Online and print articles
- Interviews
- Speeches
- Press releases
- Blogs
- Newsletters
- Screenplays, scripts, and TV shows
- Personal or professional bios
- Case studies
- Tech-related instructions or how-to manuals
- White papers and other business presentations
- Emails and text messages (or other communications)
- Social media content
- Toasts (wedding, engagements, eulogies, and congratulatory speeches)

Note: Some people are paid to ghostwrite high school or college entrance essays, which is highly discouraged since it's considered unethical. If the student applying gets caught, there can be severe consequences, likely including not being accepted or allowed to enroll. Others hire ghostwriters to write their high school or college papers and do their coursework. This is also considered cheating, and if caught, those students are most often expelled. There are currently no legal ramifications for the ghostwriter in these instances, but again, these types of work are considered extremely unethical and a quick way to stain your reputation as a writer. **10/10 do not recommend.**

WHAT MAKES SOMEONE A GREAT GHOSTWRITER?

Contrary to popular belief, you do not have to be formally trained to become a ghostwriter. It is something you can ease your way into if you have the right skill set. Great candidates for ghostwriting are those who have worked with manuscripts in some capacity, whether as a proofreader, editor, or marketer, and those who are naturally gifted at crafting clear, coherent narratives.

Your communication skills must be stellar, you must be able to receive and incorporate feedback, and you need the ability to work well with others. You must also be able to capture your client's voice and vision while adapting to a wide range of genres and subjects.

There is an art to writing well. Some people have an innate talent that is easily sharpened, while others can develop into better writers through practice, education, and constructive feedback.

So, can you become a successful ghostwriter if you've never written much of anything before and writing, grammar, and syntax aren't exactly your strengths? With lots of practice and guidance and a strong relationship with an excellent editor, you can definitely learn how to write well and build a thriving career.

HOW DO YOU GET INTO GHOSTWRITING?

Starting a career as a ghostwriter requires you to hone your writing skills so you can effectively communicate the heartbeat of a story. Begin by building a diverse portfolio of short pieces (think single chapters) that you can send as a representation of your work. Consider setting up profiles on online platforms such as Upwork and Fiverr, and enhance your LinkedIn profile to showcase your work. Network with authors, editors, and industry professionals to find potential clients. Online freelance platforms can offer initial opportunities. Our best advice is to be creative and open to the opportunities that come your way.

CREDIT OR NO CREDIT, THAT IS THE QUESTION

We're going to be straight up with you: if you choose to go down this path, there will be books for which you'll receive no credit. Zilch. Nada. Not even a mention in the acknowledgements or a small note on the copyright page.

For some books, you will be asked to sign a Non-Disclosure Agreement (NDA), and no one will ever know you've written the book. Sure, you can allude to it in your portfolio with general statements like, "I wrote a book for a well-known TED speaker who founded an organic makeup line." But you won't be able to add it to your author page on Amazon or Goodreads.

This can be a hard pill to swallow at first. It's natural to want credit for your work. However, keep in mind that's why you're eventually going to get paid the big bucks. You're essentially selling your talent. That may sound harsh, but it's no different from working at a corporate job where you give credit for your work to the organization. That PowerPoint you created for your boss to present? Or when your team wrote an entire proposal without a single mention of any individual's name? It's not all that different from ghostwriting.

As you become more established—and depending on the author and your level of involvement in the project—you may be given credit as the editor, co-author, or creative consultant, either on the copyright page or in the acknowledgements section. In cases like these, you can shout your credited involvement from the rooftops and stick that puppy right in your portfolio.

There's also the "with" and "and" credit paradigm. You'll see this often with celebrity memoirs. Essentially, "with" means the ghostwriter most likely did the bulk of the work, while "and" indicates a truly collaborative relationship in which both the author and ghostwriter made significant contributions throughout the writing process.

If this whole credit thing really bothers you, you can choose to work only with clients who will give "with" or "and" credit. But you must be okay with the fact that this may mean turning down projects that could be lucrative.

Even if you don't get "and" or "with" credit, you could request special permission from the author to list the project on your website, share writing samples with future clients, use them as a reference, or include the project in your marketing content.

TAKE ACTION

Top 5 Questions People Ask Ghostwriters

1. Does ghostwriting mean you write about ghosts?

   Nope! Not unless a client's story involves an element of the supernatural.

2. Is ghostwriting legal?

   Yes! It's legal and quite common.

3. What's the difference between writing and ghostwriting?

   The key difference is that in traditional writing, the credited author creates their own work. In ghostwriting, the credited author collaborates with a ghostwriter who takes their ideas and stories and uses their own skills to craft a polished piece.

4. Doesn't it suck when you don't receive credit?

   It's just part of the job! Plus, it doesn't hurt that we are paid well.

5. How do you choose your clients/get paired with someone?

   Most of our clients find us through referrals, Google searches, or editorial matchmaking services.

CHAPTER 3

Switching Careers Responsibly or Starting After College

There are certainly benefits to corporate life: a guaranteed paycheck, insurance through your organization, built-in community and events, predictable hours and routine (mostly), and the fact that you don't have to set up everything we just mentioned on your own. For structure junkies, this works well, and you'll probably excel at climbing that corporate ladder—until you inevitably decide to switch over to freelancing (wink-wink).

However, if you're a corporate person who is already on the precipice of leaving, don't peace out just yet. If you've been in a related career, you might have some writing samples and a good professional network, but a jump is still a jump and a risk is still a risk. Leaving your job the right way, if possible, is important, and we have some thoughts on what that looks like.

DECIDING TO LEAVE YOUR CORPORATE JOB

First, you're going to want to gather everything from your current job that might be pertinent once you head out on your own. We're not talking about staplers and post-it notes; we're talking about writing samples.

Obviously, you can't take anything proprietary (let's not do anything illegal here), but remember that when you walk out, you lose access to everything on your computer. So, start gathering any emails, files, connections, and phone numbers that may be useful to your ghostwriting future and keep them safe on your home computer. Again, do not put yourself at risk by taking anything you know you shouldn't.

During this process, you need to take a good, hard look at your financial situation. What are your expenses? How much do you need each month to cover your basic living costs? Multiply that by six. That's the amount you should have in savings before you quit your day job. Hopefully, you'll never have to touch it, but leaving a steady paycheck behind to strike out on your own lends itself to a certain level of anxiety only an adequate emergency fund can alleviate. It's important to plan for the possibility of coming up short while you build your business. Make sure you have that money saved.

You also want to include a budget in that number for setting yourself up for success through branding, creating a website, networking, attending conferences, etc. You may have to start small, but don't worry, you don't have to invest in everything upfront. Still, you'll want to have some key components of your business set up in some way before you dive in. We recommend starting with a strong website that showcases your services. This way, you'll be ready to find clients and have a professional online presence from day one.

If you're just starting out, come up with a loose, step-by-step plan on how you're going to make this happen. You might start with very small goals like, "In the first month, I'm going to secure one project that will pay out $2,000." You might give yourself some step-by-step tasks, like what to include in your pre-quitting business setup. (FYI: We've included an organizer to help you do this at the end of the chapter!)

Another thing that can help greatly is if you can start freelancing before you leave your company. If you have the bandwidth, start looking for opportunities and land one (this is what Alee did). If you can leapfrog your way out of your position with at least one paying client waiting for you on the other side, it's business rocket fuel. The money is great, of course, but as you build a resume with relevant experience, you are bound to get more work. Experience is experience, whether you're full-time or not.

STARTING RIGHT OUT OF COLLEGE

If you're coming right out of college, the situation is a bit different, though some of the same steps apply. You still need to assess your financial situation, make a plan, and budget, but this step will likely be projection-based for most recent graduates.

More than anything, you must be genuinely hungry, and that hunger needs to translate into drive. Knowing that your long-term goal is to earn income through ghostwriting will push you to take all the short-term steps necessary to get you there.

Something we're often asked by college students is, "How do I get the job if I don't have the experience?" and "What if nobody will give me work because I don't have writing samples?" While Chapter 9 goes into detail on all the ways you can create a portfolio and writing samples (read: Your classmates and friends probably have stories to tell), we do want to put something out there—a word to the wise, shall we say. Please do not send potential clients your academic papers as writing samples. If you took a creative writing class, sure, those papers could be helpful. But don't send someone your paper on the themes of sadomasochism in Poe's *The Tell-Tale Heart* or that psychology paper you wrote about the connection between nutrition and mental wellness, unless you're trying to ghostwrite literature reviews and psych papers.

Samples are important, no doubt, but if you want to start strong while figuring things out, you need to network. Take a minute to think about your professors who understand what you're doing, believe in you, and could potentially help. We can't emphasize enough the power of connection and networking.

Speaking of networking, here's an exercise to help you overcome any shyness: pretend to be someone else! As a ghostwriter, you'll need to do this anyway, so you might as well start now. When you're nervous about having a conversation or making a request, pretend to be someone extremely confident and just go for it. When it's over, you'll realize you have not, in fact, died of awkwardness. Putting yourself out there can be painful, yes—we know the struggle—but the sooner you push past the timidity, the better.

The second tip to overcoming awkward feelings or shyness in networking situations is to remember that people love being asked questions. This shifts the focus off you. When you ask advice from a professor or connect with an author whose work you admire, it's validating for them and gives you more to talk about.

Alice: The Power of Internships

If you're still in school or coming out of college, I believe you should do everything you can to land an internship in a related field. It can make a big difference and help advance your career. Whether it's during your senior year or afterward (like me!), if you know you want to be a writer, pursue a related internship. Not only will you gain experience you can tout, but you'll also meet people to add to your personal network. Trust me, these connections are like gold as you advance in your career. They can unlock opportunities, send you referrals, and maybe even become future collaborators, so make the most of every introduction.

CHOOSE YOUR CONFIDANTS WISELY

We know you've got this dream. You know you've got this dream. We believe in you. You believe in yourself. But let's be real: There are people in your life who might not support you because they can't see your vision. You might already be dreading a conversation about it with your friends and family. You'll say you're going to quit your job to write, and they'll respond with something like, "You are a freaking idiot, and you are going to lose everything you own." It's not nice, but many of us have heard something similar from haters.

So, here's the thing: You need to carefully assess who you share your dreams with. If you think one of your friends is going to freak out, don't tell them about it until things are set in motion. Share your plan sparingly. Though few people truly understand writing, most people still have opinions about creative professions, regardless of whether they're qualified to assess them.

Consider the people who'll drain your energy and by constantly pushing a "can't" narrative, because mindset can be contagious. Whether you buy into a "can't" or "can" mindset, your way of thinking can become a self-fulfilling prophecy. Success is only impossible if you don't push yourself or if you accept "no" as an answer.

Instead of letting the toxic voices of naysayers into the mix, surround yourself with the right people—and by "right," we mean people who inspire you, push you to strive, and support your growth.

It's amazing to be surrounded by people with a similar growth and positivity mindset, because when you're down, someone will lift you up without hesitation, coming from the same place. Find your people and do that for each other. Build a team of creatives you can call in the middle of the day and say, "I literally feel like I'm going to die today," and know they'll respond, "You're not going to die—go eat some chocolate."

(Alice) The Thing About English Degrees

I don't think we can close this chapter without addressing a question that's on everyone's mind: Do you need an English degree, master's degree, or some other fancy credential to write professionally? If you want a job in a publishing house, then yes, it's important to have a related degree, whether in English, literature, publishing, or journalism. However, if your goal is to freelance, the answer is a resounding NO!

I don't have a master's degree, and my English degree is technically one of three minors adjacent to a liberal arts degree. I don't even think a journalism program existed at my university when I attended. For my minor, I took poetry classes and read 18th and 19th-century literature. These classes taught me how to write a paper correctly and do research, but I certainly didn't learn the art of writing a full-length manuscript there.

Other people recognized my talent before I did. I have had a gift for writing from a young age, and others helped nurture it. Recently, my mom brought me an old "Letter to the Editor" I wrote to our local newspaper when I was eight years old. I didn't need to major in writing to be a writer; I simply needed to continue writing. My creative writing matured organically over time and with practice.

Maybe you journal like I do. The consistent practice of writing is embedded in this routine. Maybe you were the person all your friends turned to for help with their papers in college. That's coaching and critical thinking, both vital parts of the craft. Maybe you've toyed with blogging, writing plays, or composing poems. These things don't add up to an English degree, but they all enhance your writing and storytelling abilities.

Sure, your compositions probably won't be without error (neither are mine), and you may wonder if you'll ever succeed in ghostwriting. But do you want to know something about the writers who are beyond good? A secret about the "greats," those writers our English professors idolize? Mary Shelley, Stephen King, John Steinbeck, you name the legend—none of these people were born with a pen in their hand and a thesaurus for a brain. They had editors.

Take John Steinbeck, for instance. There's a long history of multiple editors pulling apart Steinbeck's work and revising it. They believed in him and helped him become better. The same goes for Ernest Hemingway and Margaret Atwood. It just takes time, determination, dedication to the craft, and a great editor— not necessarily an English degree.

Alee: On Becoming a Writer

On a slightly different note, I wasn't that kid. I didn't write to magazines or put myself out there. I was shy and too afraid of my father's critiques to try anything that bold. So, it's also not a requirement to have been living and breathing writing your whole life to achieve success as a ghostwriter. I was someone who journaled and wrote poetry from a young age, but I didn't consider myself a writer until much later in life.

I wasn't an excellent academic student, but I'm good at the parts of writing that matter for a career in writing. Yes, I do have a degree in writing, literature, and publishing, but I know plenty of great writers with master's degrees in business or other unrelated fields. People get caught up in thinking education is the be-all and end-all, but once you get past your first job or two, no one cares what your degree is as long as you have the skills.

It is my firm belief that writing is a baked-in talent. It's either something you have or something you don't. It is hard to teach, and perhaps because of this, people feel afraid of the title "writer." I say, screw that. If you write poetry "just for you," you are a writer. If you religiously updated your LiveJournal during your years of teenage angst, you are a writer. If you blog about makeup, travel, or your collection of cookie jars, you are a writer. If you've written a single short story, essay, or poem, you are a writer.

A huge part of all this is having the confidence to call yourself a writer and speak about your talent openly and respectfully. Your talent deserves to be honored. Your skill set deserves to be celebrated.

TAKE ACTION

Baby Business Brainstorm

Starting a business from scratch isn't for the faint of heart, but getting organized is a good place to start. Use the structure below to create a plan for yourself and make this happen.

MONEY	
What is your pre-business savings goal (a.k.a., your emergency fund)?	How much can you realistically set aside each month toward this goal?
CONNECTIONS	
Make a list of potential connections (e.g., entrepreneurs, business owners, CEOs, speakers, lawyers).	What non-proprietary files or information might be helpful to keep (e.g., contacts, calendar dates for conferences/events)?
TIMELINE	
When can I realistically leave my job or kickstart a side business (e.g., after saving six months' worth of expenses)?	Are there any major blocks I should consider (e.g., birth of a child, medical/health concerns or procedures, desire to purchase or refinance a home)?
MILESTONES	
Baby Business Goal #1: (e.g., Alee: Make $55,000 a year; Alice: match and exceed corporate income)	**Baby Business Goal #2:** (e.g., sign your first contract or get your first project)

CHAPTER 4

Ghostwriting and the Editing Continuum

Not all writers are editors, and not all editors are writers.

If your goal is to be a writer but you're not a trained editor, you may want to focus on projects that require you to write the entire manuscript, rather than taking on already written works that need heavy revision and editing. However, as a writer aiming to build a lucrative career, you should recognize the importance of editing and the writing-editing partnership.

Terms like "developmental editing," "substantive editing," "copyediting," and "proofreading" are thrown around all over—in the industry, social media, blogs, and on the internet at large. Sometimes, these terms are used interchangeably, but sometimes, the same term can mean entirely different things. They often blur together and can be difficult to parse out, even for established writers, let alone someone just starting out.

This means you will often field questions from clients about the differences between writing and editing. It also means that, as a writer, you need to be abundantly clear about what you're being hired to do—what that includes and what it *does not*. Be thorough in your manuscript or project assessment as well as in your quote or bid to the author, and ask plenty of questions! It's possible (even likely) that you'll have a better sense of what the project needs or what an existing manuscript requires than some authors will.

For instance, authors with an existing manuscript might ask for a **proofread** when they need a **copyedit**. Or they may request a **copyedit** when a **substantive** or **developmental edit** is required before reaching that stage. Sometimes, you'll receive a manuscript for proofreading that needs to be completely rewritten to be marketable and coherent.

At least a few times in your career, a potential client will offer to write a portion of the manuscript to save money, but you know you'll have to rewrite everything they send you anyway. Oof. It's your job as a ghostwriter to understand the differences between all these types of editorial tasks so you can assess your client's needs and provide resources for any services you don't offer.

In our own discussions of how to explain writing and editing terms, even we had to define the details of the terms we each use to ensure we were talking about the same type of editing. But never fear! We've broken down the stages of manuscript development and defined each one (along with some potential alternates) for you, so you don't have to figure it out on your own.

STAGES OF A MANUSCRIPT AND DEFINED TERMS

Writing

Simply put, writing is putting the words down—when an author puts pen to paper or fingers to keys and bares their soul for the world to see in its rawest form. As a ghostwriter, this is what you will most often be hired to do on behalf of your client.

Ghostwriting

When a writer (you'll often be referred to as either a "work-for-hire" contractor or "writer" in contracts) records and transcribes the words of the credited author and turns them into a compelling narrative for marketing, entertainment, and/or informational purposes. This includes outlining, interviewing, and research, in addition to the task of writing. When the author contributes a significant portion of the content, this is also known as **collaborating** or **co-authoring**.

Developmental Edit

This type of editing focuses on providing big-picture feedback, such as identifying plot holes, character issues, and organizational problems. It includes placing comments throughout the manuscript, but the editor/ghostwriter makes no sentence-level changes. This is ideal for authors who feel they can revise and edit on their own if given specific instructions. Typically, a one- or two-page letter is included with this service, breaking down the overarching issues. This process is also known as **DE**, or a **developmental review**.

Substantive Edit

Similar to a developmental edit, a substantive edit focuses on big-picture feedback, but also incorporates elements of detailed work. Unlike a developmental edit, this type of edit includes the editor/ghostwriter making the actual changes in the manuscript (e.g., structural, line, or otherwise) in addition to making high-level suggestions. Did you use the same word four times in one paragraph? An editor will notice and make the changes. Is there something missing or confusing? They'll fix it, or at least tell you to. This is also known as a **structural edit** or **content edit**.

Copy Edit

When it's time to zoom in and focus on particulars like grammar, word choice, sentence structure, verb tense, fact-checking, and punctuation, a manuscript is ready for a copy edit. At this stage, the editor may still provide some feedback on major issues, but traditionally, a copy edit is more focused on sentence-level details.

Line Edit

Sitting somewhere between a substantive edit and a copy edit, a line edit is a type of editing that focuses on improving the flow, clarity, and style of writing at the sentence and paragraph levels. It's more detailed than a developmental edit but less granular than a copy edit. Sometimes folks confuse this with copyediting, so if you are asked to do a line edit, always clarify the scope of work.

Typesetting

When a manuscript is deemed ready, it is sent to a designer (typesetter), who lays out the page design and flows the manuscript into a template. You'll most commonly receive the typeset pages as a PDF.

Proofreading

When a manuscript has been typeset, it needs to be checked one more time for errors in spelling, punctuation, and issues that may have been missed in earlier edits or introduced during the typesetting process. This includes extra spaces, word stacks (where the same word begins or ends a line as the one above or below, causing visual distraction), formatting inconsistencies, missing or out-of-order page numbers, etc. A proofread is sometimes done before typesetting and after to ensure as many errors as possible are caught.

THE WRITER-EDITOR ROLES AND RELATIONSHIP

Both of us were professional editors, so we know both sides of the writer-editor relationship. To start, let's be real—writers have creative juices in spades, but some of us really struggle with things like spelling, punctuation, and formatting dialogue. This is all okay. It is, after all, the editor's role to have the education and expertise to help with this. However, you can learn from these relationships to create cleaner manuscripts.

As a ghostwriter, your job is to get words on paper, be creative, follow your client's wishes, and honor their voice. But your job is *not* to get everything absolutely correct the first time. And while writer-editor relationships can be challenging, they don't have to be. You're on the same team, working to make someone's story the best it can be.

As you read this book, you'll notice we repeatedly emphasize the theme of communication and relationships. This is one of those times. A great relationship with an editor not only allows you to leverage both of your strengths, but it can also help you learn and become an even better writer. Make love with your editors, not war.

Alee: For the Love of Em-dashes

A couple of years ago, I worked with an editor who pointed out that I had used em dashes a million times in a manuscript. They told me that using em-dashes constantly watered down their overall effect. I've kept this in my head ever since, and I don't use one now unless it is truly necessary. I also make sure to tell new editors that I tend to be a little em-dash obsessed so they can look out for it. Seriously—I almost never use them. Like—almost never.

FINDING A PROFESSIONAL EDITOR

While you'll no doubt pride yourself on delivering clean manuscripts to your clients, you should never be the only set of eyes on a book you write. Before you send a batch of first-draft chapters to a client, read through everything again, then spellcheck it in Microsoft Word, and then run it through another site like Grammarly.

There will probably still be errors. At this stage of initial drafted chapters, things always get missed, even into the proofreading stages.

Once the author has approved the final draft of the manuscript, it's time to hire a professional copyeditor to review it again. You can really improve your writing by learning from the copyediting mistakes.

You'll also encounter clients who are all too happy to point out errors in the initial drafts, to which you can respond, "Thank you very much. There will be some errors while we're in the process of writing. I do my best to try to present a clean manuscript, but there will always be things I miss, which is why I send it to a professional editor after the manuscript is finished."

Finding an editor with whom you collaborate well can take some searching, but it's worth the effort. Google is your friend. We have had success reaching out to editorial groups on social media. Since we have experience in publishing, we've used our professional networks to find people who complement us, and who have the skills and obsession with writing rules we don't possess.

Finding a few people you trust in this realm is a must. A great editor will help you become an even better writer.

TAKE ACTION

Be a Writer Editors Love

Editors live by style guides. Every publisher and agency either follows an existing one or has customized their own. Essentially, a style guide is the bible for all the nitty-gritty parts of writing in particular genres and publications, ensuring consistency. They answer questions like: *Should I use a semicolon or an em-dash? Do I use the Oxford comma when writing lists? Should I avoid contractions?* And every other question you could possibly have about the "how" parts of writing.

If you want to get those editor points (and save yourself extra work), definitely ask about style guides. Want to be even more legit? Be familiar with some of the mainstays:

CHICAGO MANUAL OF STYLE (CMOS OR CMS)

This is the primary style guide for publishing long-form fiction and creative nonfiction books—so, start here! If you don't want to buy a new copy every year, consider subscribing to the online version.

Associated Press (AP Style)

If you're in short-form writing (e.g., journalism, news writing) or even biographical texts, this will be your best friend.

American Psychological Association (APA)

Thinking about getting into more technical writing? APA is used for writing in social sciences, business, and engineering.

Christian Manual of Style (CMOS)

For books involving Christian themes, this style guide is your bible (get it?)

American Medical Association (AMA)

The default writing manual for health, medicine, and biology—the go-to for the science types.

CHAPTER 5

Office Setup + Tools of the Trade

As a professional writer, you're going to spend a lot of time on your computer. Like, a *lot*. And as much as you might envision doing a Tour de Local Coffee Shops, you will probably end up banging out most of your work at home. Here's the truth: working hunched over the kitchen counter or balancing your laptop on a pillow in bed will only work for a limited time—otherwise, you're asking the universe for back problems and migraines. It's important to find ways to separate yourself from work. Personal spaces become even more important when life and work overlap (and they always do).

While it's great if you have the space, your office doesn't need to be its own room. All you need is a dedicated place in your home as your workstation—the spot where you keep all your work things.

To figure this out, you might need to get creative! Is there a corner of your kitchen or living room where you can fit a computer desk? Do you have a closet you could turn into a usable space? Is there room in your garage for a table and chairs and does it have good Wi-Fi reception? Whatever it is, create some physical boundaries and a place to keep your belongings organized.

OFFICE MUST-HAVES

- Computer and a cable/Wi-Fi subscription
- Webcam for video calls (if not built into computer)
- Microsoft Word
- Zoom subscription or other video call platform
- Printer
- Notebook
- Pens/Pencils
- Digital audio recording device
- Time tracking and invoicing software like Clockify or Harvest

OFFICE NICE-TO-HAVES

- Noise-canceling headphones
- Blue light glasses
- Lamp
- Highlighters
- Post-it notes
- Printed copy of Webster's Dictionary
- Printed copy of Chicago Manual of Style (most recent edition)
- Printed Thesaurus
- Books in different trim sizes for reference

HELPFUL SOFTWARE AND WEBSITES

- Dropbox (for storing files)
- Google Drive (for storing files) and Google Docs (for writing)

- Grammarly (for correcting grammar)
- Rev.com (for transcribing recorded interviews)
- Fireflies.ai (for cataloging and transcribing interviews via video call)
- Docusign (for securely sending and signing contracts)

PREP YOUR SPACE FOR VIDEO CALLS

As you set up your office space, it's vital to keep in mind that much of your client work will take place via video calls. This means ensuring you have an optimal setup, with a clutter-free background and privacy from kids, partners, and pets, a clutter-free background (please do not take video calls in front of your unmade bed).

If possible, position yourself facing a natural light source or use a lamp or ring light. If your computer doesn't have a built-in camera, invest in a quality webcam and microphone for clear audio and video. Remember, you'll need to capture the audio of your calls, so be sure to use a platform with that capability. Our favorite is Zoom.

GATHER THINGS YOU LOVE

Writing can be highly emotional, and operating your business can be stressful. This is why it's important to have things in your workspace that make you feel safe, calm, and inspired. Consider adding photos of your family, candles, plants, squishy things to play with, and even a dedicated space for an iPad or Kindle if you like to have a show streaming in the background (ahem, Alee). If there's space, add a bookshelf, stock it with books that inspire you—and plan to stock a shelf (or three) with books you've worked on! Treat your workspace like a sanctuary. After all, you'll be running the world from that desk in no time.

TAKE ACTION

Create Your Office

Once you choose a location, your next task is to create the look and feel that will work best for you. Consider both functionality and form. You'll need to produce work consistently, so practicality is important, but what can you add that inspires you? Consider how you can repurpose things you already have or make an inexpensive trip to your local dollar store or thrift store. Research Pinterest and TikTok for organizational hacks, and figure out what you need to purchase to set up your physical space.

You can keep pens and pencils in mason jars, flower vases, or toothbrush holders. Enjoy fishing? Use an old tackle box as a storage container for your desk gadgets. A plastic upright dish drainer can hold file folders, and you can spray paint just about anything to add some color to your desk space.

First, make a list of all your necessities, then draw up your office plan!

MY NECESSITIES

-
-
-
-
-
-
-

MY OFFICE SPACE

CHAPTER 6

Building Your Team of Professional Service Providers

Let's talk about setting up your business *the right way.* The great thing about owning your own business is you're the one in charge. However, the challenging thing about owning a business is that *you're the one in charge.* No one else is handling your insurance or business registration. No one is there to take the taxes out of your paycheck. No one is there to pay your salary or drum up business. It's all on you.

Being an entrepreneur means you're the captain of your ship, responsible for keeping the whole damn thing afloat, which means you'll wear many hats. You'll be the administrator, sales manager, CFO, and CEO, as well as the writer, admin, and project manager. If that sounds overwhelming, don't worry. Setting yourself up properly and getting the right people in place will make it all flow beautifully even before you put pen to paper.

BUILDING YOUR SUPPORT TEAM

While you can certainly start your freelance ghostwriting career flying solo, having the right professionals in your corner from early on will set you up for smoother operations and faster growth. Both Alice and Alee started with the basics—lawyers and Certified Public Accountants (CPAs)—and expanded their teams as their businesses took off. Regardless of your situation, you're stepping into a career that will sometimes make you feel out of your league. You'll want a team in place faster than you think!

LEGAL + FINANCIAL HELP

Let's think about this critically. As you begin to build your business, the very first thing you're working toward is landing a client relationship. And when this happens, you need a solid contract in place and a plan regarding the financial end of things (e.g., How will you take payments? How will you take out taxes? How will you pay yourself?). When you're just starting out, having a lawyer draft your initial contract template is invaluable. This helps you avoid loopholes and missing clauses in contracts that are auto-generated by websites.

Unless you genuinely enjoy wrestling with tax forms and messing with numbers, hiring a bookkeeper and CPA is key. These professionals are highly qualified to keep your finances organized and compliant, which means you'll avoid the pitfalls of late tax payments and missed invoices from the get-go. Contrary to what you may believe, these aren't luxuries—they're strategic investments in your business's foundation that will pay for themselves through the money they save you.

When looking for both, we highly suggest seeking out personal recommendations from people you trust. We have both gotten stuck in situations where we've found people via Google search who were qualified on paper but just didn't work out because of mismatched expectations, crappy communication, or a lack of experience in our industry. Try reaching out to your favorite writing networking group or your local community Facebook page. Be specific about exactly what you are looking for, such as capabilities and personality. The more detailed you are upfront, the better your chances are of finding someone you can trust and want to partner with.

ADMINISTRATIVE SUPPORT

As your workload increases, a Virtual Assistant (VA) will make your life so much easier. A skilled VA can become indispensable, helping you juggle multiple roles by managing your calendar, handling bookkeeping tasks, tracking project statuses, sending deadline reminders, and assisting with invoicing. The good news? VAs aren't prohibitively expensive—most of them serve several professionals at once, so they're not counting on you alone to provide them enough hours to live on.

For more complex operations, a Project Manager (PM) can be a game-changer! They excel at maintaining detailed task lists for each client and project, managing editorial workflows, serving as client liaisons, and fielding incoming leads. A VA and PM can be the same person as long as that individual is highly organized and eager to be involved.

OTHER THINGS TO CONSIDER

As your business expands, think about these other areas where hiring professional help might be worth the investment:

- Marketing support: Will you invest in paid advertising? Consider how much you'll spend, how frequently, and through which channels.

- Social media assistance: Do you want help building a professional presence or creating and publishing content regularly?

- Website design: A professional web presence can significantly impact client acquisition and make it easier for you to highlight your portfolio and services.

- Business consultation: Having advisors for both small daily decisions and major strategic choices.

- Contract maintenance: Regular reviews and updates to your agreements (your lawyer can suggest what clauses might be necessary).

Remember, you control the pace. Decide what works best for your situation and budget, striking a balance with your immediate needs and long-term benefits.

TAX IDENTIFICATION AND BUSINESS STRUCTURE

You'll need to decide whether to use your Social Security Number (SSN) on tax documents or obtain an Employer Identification Number (EIN). In the USA, your state's Small Business Administration (SBA) website typically provides the process details.

Your choice of business structure—sole proprietorship, Limited Liability Company (LLC), or S-Corp—will determine the paperwork you need to complete, fees you'll pay, and requirements you must meet. Each structure has different implications for taxes, liability, and operations.

Contact the appropriate government offices, consult with your CPA, and talk to your lawyer about the best business structure for your specific situation. Learn your state's requirements thoroughly and find professionals licensed in your state to advise you—then, actually listen to their guidance.

If something feels off about the advice you're receiving, or if a professional doesn't have the patience to answer your questions thoroughly, seek a second opinion. In fact, always plan on getting a second opinion for major business decisions.

Alice: Why I Chose an LLC

For most of my career, I operated as a sole proprietor, which meant I only had an EIN. After discussions with both my lawyer and my accountant, they felt there was no benefit for me to change, as the legalities of a sole proprietorship in Tennessee are similar to those of an LLC.

In 2019, though, I decided to become an LLC. It symbolized an upleveling of my business, and I wanted to explore additional passive income streams. I also felt that having "LLC" on legal documents and contracts looked more professional than just using my name.

Alee: On Being a Sole Proprietor

Thirteen years into my freelance career, I am still a sole proprietor. Truthfully, I don't necessarily have a strategic reason for this other than my lawyer, CPA, and I haven't come up with a compelling reason to switch to an LLC, and so I haven't. At the end of each year, examine where you are vs. where you want to be, and assess what you need to do (or not do) to move toward your goals. The key lesson here is to always be evaluating and reevaluating.

PRACTICAL CONSIDERATIONS

Consider these operational elements as you establish your business:

- Do you need business cards?

- Should you obtain professional liability insurance?

- How will you handle different payment methods? Do you know how to receive bank wires or process credit cards if clients prefer those options?

- How often should you review and update your contracts?

Insurance

In addition to health, life, car, and home/renters' insurance, you might consider disability insurance and Errors & Omissions (E&O) insurance. E&O insurance protects you against claims of inadequate work or negligent actions. However, if you have a solid contract (ahem, lawyer), this may not be necessary. Please contact your legal professional for specific advice in this area.

Savings

If you have children or plan to have them, parental leave as a freelancer is nonexistent unless you've saved for it. So, you're going to need a plan. Essentially, it's a savings goal. Look at your budget and expenses. *How much* are you going to need? *How long* are you going to take off? Should you plan for a buffer period as you start to pick up clients again? Will you maintain the same client load as you did before having children? Big questions, we know, but they need to be answered ahead of time.

The same principles of saving and planning apply to your retirement fund, investing, donating, and wealth management. You've got to make money management a priority. Unless you have a working spouse or partner, you're the only one "matching" contributions—because the only contributions are from you. Enjoy the wealth you accumulate, but make sure to save enough to stay safe and comfortable now and in the future.

MAKING SMART DECISIONS

Balance what you can afford right now with what will benefit you most in the long term. When spending a little extra money upfront will save you significant time, stress, or money later, carefully weigh those decisions. Choose what's best for your specific situation, keeping both immediate constraints and future growth in mind. Setting up your business properly from the start isn't just about checking boxes—it's about creating a foundation that will support your growth and protect your interests as you build your career. While it might feel overwhelming to think about lawyers, accountants, business structures, and virtual assistants when you're just getting started, remember that you don't need to have everything in place on day one. The key is knowing that there are resources available when you need them.

ONE STEP AT A TIME

Start with the essentials: a solid contract template, a basic understanding of your tax obligations, and a simple system for tracking your finances. As your client base grows and your income increases, gradually add team members and refine your business structure. The key is to stay ahead of your needs rather than scrambling to catch up.

Most importantly, don't try to figure everything out alone. The cost of professional advice from a lawyer, accountant, or business consultant is minimal compared to the potential costs of mistakes or missed opportunities. These professionals have guided countless entrepreneurs through the same decisions you're facing—let their expertise work for you.

Your business is more than just your writing skills; it's a complete professional enterprise. By investing time and resources into building it properly, you're not just protecting yourself—you're positioning yourself to thrive in a competitive industry. Take it one step at a time, get the help you need, and remember that every successful ghostwriter once sstarted from scratch.

TAKE ACTION

First Steps: Creating a Foundation for Success

We won't say there's a completely wrong way to set up your business, but you'll save yourself time and protect your sanity if you avoid taking shortcuts and do it right the first time. There are options to explore, but ultimately, there are certain steps you *must* take to create a solid, legal foundation you can build upon.

1. Business Setup

- Research and hire a lawyer to help you craft your work-for-hire contract.

- Decide on the business structure you'll use (sole proprietorship, LLC, S-Corp, etc.).

- Hire quality financial professionals to help you plan for the future, including your retirement and savings goals.

- Get an EIN.

- Open a business banking account.

- Sign up for accounting software if you plan to do this yourself.

- Research web-based programs to build your own website if you have the desire and skill set, or hire an affordable web designer.

2. Research organizations in your area that may offer free or discounted services for starting small businesses, or connect with your local chamber of commerce to help with networking, mentoring, and referral opportunities.

CHAPTER 7

Developing Your List of Offerings and Setting Your Prices

Creating a service sheet (also called a one-sheet) as a freelance writer is crucial. This document serves as a hub of information for potential clients, clearly outlining your offerings, rates, and terms. A well-designed service sheet portrays professionalism, transparency, and expertise, helping clients understand the value you provide. By using a service sheet, you can facilitate smoother negotiations, making it easier to land the deals you deserve.

You may be wondering why you need a service sheet at all. After all, as a ghostwriter, your writing is, of course, your main selling point. However, there are many ways to present your skills and experience that can enhance your offerings before you start pitching to clients.

For example, if you're a skilled project manager, you can add project management to your list; if you're an experienced proofreader, you can include that as well; and if you're well-versed in certain topics or fluent in another language, you can highlight those as areas of expertise.

DEVELOPING YOUR ELEVATOR PITCH

One of the first things you need to do is create your mission statement, so that when you meet someone looking for your services, you can clearly explain what you provide. It's not going to benefit you just to say, "I'm a writer." Your elevator pitch should be short, crystal clear, and memorable.

Alee, for example, has refined her focus to the point where she says, "I am a ghostwriter who specializes in grief and trauma." This works because it's very specific and immediately helps people understand if she's the right fit for their project. Test your pitch on friends and family, or at networking events. Pay attention to people's reactions. If they seem confused, you'll need to simplify your language. Continue refining and practicing until you can deliver it with confidence in under a minute.

CREATING A LIST OF OFFERINGS AND SERVICES

Once you have your elevator pitch, place that at the top of the sheet. Then, create a list of offerings and services with a brief description of each. Here's an example:

Example One-Sheet

Alee Anderson *is a ghostwriter who specializes in memoirs for those processing acute trauma and journeying through complex grief. Services include:*

Ghostwriting*: Writing a full manuscript up to 65,000 words.*

Rewriting*: Rewriting a client's manuscript up to 85,000 words.*

Developmental Editing*: Editing a client's manuscript up to 85,000 words.*

Project Management*: Facilitating the process from concept to publishing.*

Book Coaching*: Coaching clients in the creation of a memoir.*

CREATE YOUR STANDARD OPERATING PROCEDURES

The more upfront you can be about your standard operating procedures, the better. Some boundaries can be set automatically when someone first makes contact. For instance, some freelancers have a timeframe wherein they typically respond to inquiries, and this is posted on their website or included in an automated email response. Others have some of their guidelines baked into their contracts.

When you live and work in the same place, it's especially easy to get lax on time-related boundaries and feel like you must respond to communication immediately because your phone is always nearby. Without the physical separation between your home and workplace, the idea of a "workday" or "workweek" gets murky.

You may decide not to reply to clients after 5 p.m. or on weekends. Whatever works for you—just make sure you convey your normal work hours to your clients. And if you're contacted at 9 p.m. or on a Sunday morning, you don't have to respond unless you want to. The world won't end, and you can respond the next business day.

SET YOUR SERVICE RATES

Setting rates as a freelance writer can be tricky, and it can feel impossible to know where to start. Most of us enter freelance work by charging lower rates until we get our sea legs, then we slowly increase our fees over time. For many, this is a necessary step, especially when you recognize that the experience you gain will inevitably allow you to raise your rates.

As you begin to figure this out, consider the whole picture. Factors such as experience, expertise, industry standards, genre, timeline, and the complexity of the work all play a role in your pricing. Aim for a balance between competitive pricing and fair compensation for your work.

Start by looking at the Editorial Freelancers Association (EFA)[1] for an updated view of standard industry rates. (Please note: EFA rates are typically on the lower end.) Knowing this, you can use those rates as a baseline and then adjust accordingly based on your personal needs. Be prepared to negotiate rates with clients while maintaining confidence in the value of your services, ensuring a mutually beneficial arrangement that reflects your worth as a professional.

Another option, which we encourage you to pursue, is to ask other ghostwriters about their rates. While it may be awkward to have those conversations, it's important to power through them.

Knowledge is your friend, and it's your responsibility to look after your own best interests, raise your rates, and stay aware of market trends. A quick Google search on how much ghostwriters charge can be helpful here. When you're first starting out, you may not charge as much as someone in their fifth or fifteenth year of writing, but you might. Many seasoned ghostwriters charge a dollar or two a word, if not more.

As you break into ghostwriting and figure out pricing, it's like one of those "Choose Your Own Adventure" books that were popular in the eighties and nineties. The adventure here is how you'll break into the industry and create your personal path to financial success. Buckle your seat belts—this is where the ride gets exciting. We're going to give you the transparent, no-BS scoop about money because, well, why wouldn't we?

One of the great things about the ghostwriting community—at least the ones we're familiar with—is the support. While some careers in publishing can be cutthroat, the mindset here is a little different. There are, of course, some outliers, by and large, in the writing communities we're part of, everyone understands there's enough work for everyone. This reduces the need for ultracompetitive, secretive

---

[1] http://www.the-efa.org.

games. Instead, people provide encouragement, education, and valuable perspectives.

In the spirit of full disclosure, we must acknowledge that it's hard to guide you through this topic in extensive detail. Each person's goals, journey, and needs are unique, and your pricing will reflect that. But wherever you start, your goal should be to steadily increase your rates as you gain experience.

Alice: Why Money Conversations Matter

Early in my career, I priced everything based on what I knew about my former publishing house's freelance editing rates, which averaged between $8-14/hour in the early 2000s. This was all I knew, especially since we weren't allowed to talk about our salaries. (Damn you, Corporate America.)

About eight years into my freelance career, I asked my lawyer if my prices were remotely on-target, to which she replied, "You charge less than half of what everybody else does, and you have more experience." This is one of the only times I'll say it: "Don't be like me." Otherwise, I'm a gem.

It had never occurred to me that I could openly talk about money now that I was a freelancer. Once I realized that, I started asking around, finding out what other people charged for various types of work. I immediately raised my rates, and I've continued to do so every few years as my experience has grown. I'm a big fan of openly discussing money!

Every single one of us starts from a different place. Some people will land a $100,000 deal right out of the gate. Is that wrong? No, it's amazing. Should you aim for that? Well, it depends.

If you don't have a body of work, you might start with a smaller amount and grow from there. Many beginner ghosts charge between $15,000 and $50,000 for a book. (By the way, another useful thing to look up online is the sweet spot for word count per genre. Memoirs can range from 40,000 to 100,000+ words, while business leadership books often fall between 50,000-60,000 words.)

Perhaps you already have proof that you can do the work, and you want to charge more than the EFA suggests because your first client has a big budget. Whatever the situation, start where you're comfortable, based on your ability, needs, goals, depth of experience, and, perhaps most importantly, your confidence.

Alice: My Pricing Journey

The first two books I wrote paid around $1,200 a piece, and I was transcribing speeches from a cassette tape on my Sony Walkman. However, a fellow ghostwriter landed her very first book deal for $60,000. I know plenty of ghostwriters who have jumped right into the industry with their rates set at $75,000 per project. It's all about what the market will bear and what you have the confidence to charge—and the writing ability to sustain.

After I left the publishing house, my starting point for ghostwriting books was around $12,000. I was getting most of my projects through agencies and proving myself. After a few years (remember, every book is experience), I added $5,000 to $10,000 to my next project and continued increasing my rates until I reached a comfortable price point. Once I made it to $25,000–$30,000 per book, I waited a few more years and jumped to $50,000, then $75,000, and eventually $95,000.

> *Now, I'm solidly charging six figures, but I'll still say yes now and then to a book with a smaller budget if I know I'll have a blast working on it.*

RAISING YOUR RATES

Every single book you write adds to your experience. You don't need to wait five years, have a probationary period, or have some specific corporate structure in order to increase your rates. Every single piece of work you do adds to your value. You don't have to wait for someone else to give you a raise anymore.

For instance, 2020 was a fascinating year for both of us for many reasons, but especially financially. While it seemed like everyone around us was taking massive financial hits, we both raised our rates and doubled our previous annual incomes during this time. Part of this is because, with our current price points, our clients typically fall into higher income brackets. We reasoned that perhaps the pandemic gave them the time to reevaluate priorities and invest in creative projects. Neither one of us would have discovered this had we not raised our rates, despite the widespread warnings of a global financial crisis.

FIGURING OUT YOUR JUMPING-OFF POINT AND KNOWING YOUR WORTH

We wish there was a magic number we could tell you to start with, but it really is different for everyone. However, if you're looking for a formula, we suggest going about it one of two ways:

1. Add up your monthly expenses. Figure out what you need to make in a year and how many projects you can realistically take on.

2. Add up your current annual salary and align it with your spending. What do you currently make versus what do you know you could survive on?

One of the most important mindset shifts in this business, especially if you're transitioning from traditional employment, is recognizing that you determine your worth. We're accustomed to it being determined by salary bands, annual reviews, and budgetary caps—all things that were out of our control. We also sometimes come from a place of scarcity, whether in experience, mindset, background, or all of the above. When we start from a place of lack, it can be difficult to both assess and assert our value.

But neither of these situations applies to you anymore, Dear Writer. If you have the skills to support your growth—grow, friend, grow.

TAKE ACTION

First Steps: Starting a Freelance Writing Business

- Create your list of offerings/services.

- Research rates with the EFA.

- Review what other freelancers are charging for similar services.

- Set your service rates.

- Build an aesthetically pleasing one-sheet (we LOVE Canva for this).

- Create a website (or hire someone to do it for you).

- Make a list of everyone you know in the industry (or adjacent to the industry) and email one of these people each day and decide how often to follow-up.

- Join industry-related Facebook groups.

- Set up a social media account for your business.

CHAPTER 8

Find Your Niche and Brand to Celebrate Your Strengths

Someone once told us at an editorial meeting, "If you try to speak to everyone, you'll end up speaking to no one." Repeat this to yourself like a mantra. Write it down and post it somewhere visible. Not only are you *not* everyone's cup of tea (which you aren't), you don't want to be everyone's cup of tea. Instead, you *want* to strongly appeal to those you are most suited to serve. This way, you'll attract the clients who are your best match.

Many fear that developing a niche will hinder their ability to attract clients effectively. On the contrary, developing a niche as a freelance writer allows you to establish expertise, credibility, and marketability on a specific topic or range of topics. By specializing, you can access a distinct audience, deeply understand their needs, and offer tailored solutions. Niche specialization sets you apart from less-focused writers, enabling you to command higher rates, attract ideal clients, and build a strong brand identity. Moreover, it creates opportunities for continuous growth within your chosen area of expertise.

NICHING DOWN

When trying to establish your niche, it is important to look at the very things that make you tick. Are you deeply interested in sports, music, fashion, or something else? Do you get excited by content that is spiritual or esoteric in nature? Are you drawn to dark topics that may be difficult for clients to process? Once you identify your niche, tap into your empathic side and try to picture what this says about your audience profile. Will you work with a specific gender? Age group? Emotional state? This is all part of your niche, which will shape the foundation of your branding.

I FIGURED OUT MY NICHE, NOW WHAT?

So, you've got a good idea of your niche and have started to narrow your audience. That's a great start. Now it's time to figure out how to catch your target audience's eye. It's vision board time—but this time, the focus isn't on you; it's on your future clients.

For example, Alee's ghostwriting business is gender-neutral, and her clients, ages 35+, share difficult, highly personal stories. She's a writer who deals with the darkest of dark subject matters. The most obvious choice would be to present herself as a serious person who's there to drill down and get to the facts, right? Not quite.

> ### Alee: Serving My Niche
>
> *I spent years searching for my niche before stumbling upon it by accident. In 2017, while grappling with my father's sudden death, I joined a grief support group. Through our raw conversations about loss, dying, and trauma, I discovered something unexpected: I had a rare gift for sitting with people at the intersection of acute pain and transformative healing. I realized I could combine this ability to navigate difficult*

emotional terrain with my writing expertise to serve clients in a powerful way. Today, I meet people wherever they are in their grief journey and help them transform their deepest pain into compelling, bestselling books.

When I created a vision board for my brand, I thought about times I felt nervous or apprehensive about sharing my story. I reflected on what kind of imagery would appeal to me in that state. I went with warm imagery featuring soft colors—things that made me feel safe.

After curating my images, I looked for patterns and themes. I saw a happy sunrise, the ocean, and wildflowers. I saw inclusive, natural, muted imagery that evoked feelings of joy, hope, and peace. From there, I started to gather and plan color palettes, fonts, and photos. The resulting brand guide became the foundation for my website, social media posts, client communication—everything.

While the obvious choice might be somber, I brand with light, airy elements, and I smile in photos. I choose to be inviting because, when I think about it, the people I collaborate with need to feel comforted and confident that I'll shed light on a topic they feel has been underrepresented. I'll support them and hold their story sacred. That's what people see when they visit my website.

Your personality can enhance your brand and mission, making them even stronger. Let's say your specialty is finance books, and you're a cool chick covered in tattoos who knows her stuff. You'll stand out in the market as long as your copy is consistent, your message is solid, and you keep emphasizing the value you bring. It's important to represent your personality, and your niche must be clear. So, after creating your vision board, measure it against your revised elevator pitch and ensure every single piece of copy matches that pitch.

Keep in mind, though, that your job with your brand is only partially about selling yourself. Ultimately, you're selling a specific skill set and a solution. Your brand isn't just about staying true to yourself—it's about staying true to your message. How you deliver that message is where your personality comes into play.

No matter who you are, you want your website visitors to walk away saying, "I want to meet this person." Don't try to be a jack-of-all-trades and risk diluting your value. Be clear about your strengths and the specific things you offer. Get your name out there (Networking is Chapter 11!), and they will come.

HOW FAR DOES BRANDING REACH?

Branding isn't just about the look and feel of your website. Your branding influences everything your business touches. It should extend to your logo, which should appear in your email signature. Your email signature and the way you title yourself should be consistent. Additionally, having a professional email address that aligns with your brand is vital.

Alee:

If I were Alee Anderson Editorial with the email surfergirl1998, it would be incongruent and unprofessional. I still see people with email addresses like that. Baby girl, let it go.

Also, consider creating business cards. I like to have postcards on hand for mailers as well. Stickers with your business address and logo on them are not a bad idea either. All these elements help package your product and put a pretty bow on it.

Once you figure out your branding, you should immediately create a brand guide. I use PowerPoint slides for this. My guide covers every unique aspect of my brand, from colors and textures to fonts. I stick to it for everything I do. Then, for example, if you

---

> *hire a web designer, you can send them your brand guide as a jumping-off point.*
>
> *For my personal brand, well, let's be honest, I'm a little bit of a whackadoo. I like big, funky glasses and fun, vibrant patterns on clothes. I have tattoos, which I never intentionally cover. I'm completely myself (minus some of the shits and fucks) with every potential client I interview. I want them to be as comfortable with me as I am. I'm not about to pretend I'm somber and serious just because the subject matter I work with is dark. It's more important for me to portray myself authentically than to pander to those who just don't get me.*

The same goes for you. It's vital to present exactly who you are. Otherwise, you'll spend an insane amount of time pretending to be someone you're not. You own your brand. You are your work. It just doesn't feel good to hide that in any way. Ever since we stopped taking on clients that didn't reflect our vibe, we've felt a freedom that we're not willing to stifle anymore. We have both learned that we don't have to be quiet, soft-spoken women to garner business. Our clients hire us for exactly who we are. And your clients will hire you for the same reason.

YOUR BRAND ON SOCIAL MEDIA

Branding is vital for freelancers on social media. Like it or not, it's likely the first place a potential client is going to go to check you out. What they see could either terrify them (hello, tequila shots!) or establish recognition, trust, and differentiation in a crowded marketplace. If your branding is cohesive across platforms, it communicates professionalism and a keen attention to detail—it also makes it easier for clients to find and remember you. By developing and maintaining a compelling brand narrative, you can forge meaningful connections with potential clients, making it far easier to convert them into paying customers.

TAKE ACTION

Create a Branding Guide

Your brand guide is a document to keep on hand that clearly defines your brand's values and aesthetic. Challenge yourself to set this up in PowerPoint with inspirational words on one side, and a corresponding image on the other:

IMAGERY INSPIRATION

- Natural
- Active
- Light
- Playful
- Joyful
- Imperfect
- Organic
- Color pops

Slides to Create:

- Inspirational words (e.g., joyous, active, fun)

- Imagery feel (e.g., vibrant, bright, colorful)

- Brand colors (use Pantone's website to find coordinating colors you like)

- Font inspiration (use Adobe fonts to find fonts you like)

- Inspiration images (use the stock photo site of your choice to screenshot and copy photos)

Once you've put it all together, step back and look at it with fresh eyes. Does it represent you and the clients you want to work with? Does it feel cohesive? Share it with a friend or fellow writer and ask for their feedback. Don't be afraid to review and refine your branding as your business evolves.

CHAPTER 9

How to Create Writing Samples

It's finally time to answer the ever-present question: How do you get the job if you don't have the experience? How do you create a writing sample when no one will hire you because you don't have any writing samples? These questions pop into our DMs from professional writing hopefuls more than any others. Now that we've established you can't simply send off your college English essay to a publisher or potential client, let's explore your options.

OPTION 1: MAKE UP A STORY

As someone who cut her teeth in fiction, Alee's mind is always teeming with stories. When building her first samples, she took advantage of this and wrote something super creative, straight from the heart. The sample was around 2,500 words and worked wonders in landing her first set of clients.

OPTION 2: SET UP AN INTERVIEW

One thing we have instructed people to do is interview a classmate, family member, or friend who has a story, write it up, and present it to them. Make sure to go back and forth a couple of times, get their thoughts on your draft so you can make changes, and so on.

Here's the thing: While it's nice to be able to say, "This piece is from X publication," you can't always do that when you are starting out, for lots of reasons. However, a sample is a sample. If you can write up someone's story in a way they love (and that demonstrates your abilities), that's more important than being able to send a published link.

Remember, our business is *ghost*writing, so even established writers sometimes must get creative with samples (thank you, NDAs). Just remember, the validity of a writing sample isn't defined by whether there was a monetary exchange. It's determined by the fact that you did the damn thing.

OPTION 3: DO IT DIY STYLE

The important thing to remember about samples is that they are not your resume; they are a demonstration of your skill set. As such, they don't even have to be writing you've done for someone else.

We are capable of finding stories and writing them independently. Watch a video, read the news, find inspiration somewhere, and write something.

You can also include your writing samples on your website in the form of a blog. Alice had several magazine articles and personal blog articles to show as her first writing samples, and they worked well enough to prove that she had a natural storytelling gift.

Even though Alee had a ton of experience in publishing and editing, she entered the world of ghostwriting with few writing projects she could present as samples. Everything she had done was editing or short-form writing. To overcome these challenges at the start of her ghostwriting career, she used news stories and other sources to write sample chapters, framing them as a part of something bigger.

OPTION 4: GET PUBLISHED

Yep, you're reading that right. You really can just get published. There are websites with easy-to-meet guidelines that pretty much guarantee you'll see your name in a byline. Some of these sites will require a small fee, and that's okay. If it's important for you to point to something and say, "See! There I am!" or have titles and weblinks to add to your resume, you can absolutely make it happen (Alee owns one of these websites. It's called Hey! Young Writer. Check it out!).

I HAVE MY SAMPLES—NOW WHAT?

Alice keeps folders on her desktop with a few PDF sample chapters each for memoir, business leadership, and self-help—the three areas in which she specializes. Alee keeps a folder on her desktop containing memoirs written in many different voices to show her range.

Once you've worked on several projects, you'll be able to group your samples by genre, topic, gender, or whatever criteria a client asks for. Sometimes, a client will only want to see samples you've written for women authors; other times, they'll want to ensure you can write convincingly in a man's voice. They may also want to see how you've written for authors of different cultural and ethnic backgrounds.

LOCATION, PERMISSION, AND OTHER SAMPLE ADVICE

There are a few other things to keep in mind with your samples:

1. **Permission.** The best way to continue to grow your portfolio and collect samples is to request permission in your contract. You can offer to remove identifying information, but having the foresight to ask permission proactively is key.

2. **Format.** Do not—I repeat, do NOT—send your sample in Word format. Get them as polished and compliant with non-disclosure

agreements as possible, make sure your name and the word "sample" appear somewhere in the header or footer, and export that baby to PDF with a watermark slapped in the background. This way, no one can easily edit it, there is no risk of wonky Word issues, and you look legit.

3. **Range.** If you write both fiction and nonfiction, make sure you have samples of each. If you dabble in several genres or styles, try to showcase that range. Don't save everything you write, but do save the best of what you write. Got it?

4. **Location.** If someone asks you for a sample, make sure it's easily accessible and ready to go. Keep a folder of samples on your desktop so you can quickly pop one of them into an email. Don't wait to create a sample until you're asked for one.

5. **Proofread.** Please proofread. Hire someone to edit your samples. Pay the money. Whatever it takes. Then check them again. There is no need for you to relive Alee's I-will-never-forget-what-chair-I-was-sitting-in-when-my-resume-error-was-highlighted-for-the-room experience.

Most importantly, remind yourself that you are under no obligation to tell potential clients where your samples came from or what happened to them. In our field, it's not necessary to have a resume full of experience to create a legitimate portfolio. If it's your writing, that's what truly matters.

A lot of writers who are just starting out feel they must create perfect samples, post them on their website, and get published before they can call themselves writers or start pitching to clients. We've said it before, and we'll say it again: This is false. You already have the skills; all you need now is the confidence to take the next step.

Also, just a little side note to end this chapter: It's a myth that your samples should be posted on your website for everyone to access. Alee doesn't have that, and neither does Alice. Don't let anyone tell you otherwise.

We choose to curate our selection of samples based on each individual project bid. There's no need to show potential clients anything that doesn't pertain to their project. After all, if they happen to click first on a sample that's irrelevant, they may choose to steer clear of you altogether. No, thank you!

TAKE ACTION

10 Prompts for Writing Samples

As you consider how to craft your writing samples, we've come up with some potential inspirational prompts for you. Remember, samples aren't about who paid you, or if someone paid you at all—they're about whether you can string words together well enough for someone to hire you!

Try to write a few pages based on any of these prompts to get your creative brain going:

1. Little did they know . . .

2. After years of denying myself, I began to take ownership of my sexuality. The problem was he/she/they were there, waiting to do the same.

3. An explosion below. Metal clanging. Stars racing toward me. My heart slamming. My mind racing, then blank. Weightless. Above me, I saw . . .

4. It was the greatest night of my life . . .

5. Setting: Woodstock 1979.

6. The trip was transformative. I saw qualities in myself I never knew I possessed, namely . . .

7. I'd never experienced true shock until . . .

8. They told me what I'd done. I searched my mind. No memories came.

9. She walked up to him and asked, "Have we met before?"

10. No one could have anticipated that a single comment could cause such division, anger, and anguish. What I meant to say was . . .

CHAPTER 10

Learn About Publishing Options

When generating your first leads, you've got to prepare yourself for the conversations you will inevitably have. Though most of your early discussions will center on process and your personal business practices, potential clients will also have plenty of questions about publishing and what you believe the best route for them would be. Although you'll want to do extensive research about publishing on your own, here is a broad overview of publishing options with the strengths and weaknesses of each:

TRADITIONAL PUBLISHING

Traditional publishing involves authors submitting book proposals and manuscripts to literary agents who will choose to represent an author if they believe the book proposal (and manuscript) is solid and saleable. Then, the agent's job is to pitch the book proposal to traditional publishing houses, which then select, edit, produce, and distribute the work. The literary agents will typically negotiate contracts on behalf of authors. Traditional publishers handle editing, cover design, printing, marketing, and distribution, relieving authors of these responsibilities.

One significant benefit of traditional publishing is the prestige and credibility it offers. Books published by established houses often receive wider recognition and distribution, leading to increased visibility and potential sales. Authors also benefit from professional editing, design, and marketing support, which enhances the quality and marketability of their work.

However, traditional publishing has its drawbacks. Authors face fierce competition, with only a fraction of submitted manuscripts being accepted for publication. The process can be lengthy, often taking years from manuscript submission to book release. Additionally, authors may have limited control over aspects such as cover design, pricing, and marketing strategies. Despite these challenges, traditional publishing remains a sought-after option for authors aspiring to a wide readership and professional validation.

HYBRID (CUSTOM) PUBLISHING

Hybrid (otherwise known as custom) publishing blends aspects of traditional and self-publishing models (discussed next), offering authors a middle ground between the two. Authors typically pay for some publishing services but also benefit from professional editorial, design, and distribution support. Unlike traditional publishing, where manuscripts are selected by the publisher, hybrid publishers often accept a wider range of genres and authors, allowing for more diverse voices and stories to reach the market.

One significant benefit of hybrid publishing is the combination of editorial expertise and authorial control. Authors retain creative input while accessing professional publishing services, which improves the quality of the final product. Additionally, hybrid publishers often offer wider distribution channels and marketing support compared to self-publishing alone.

However, hybrid publishing can be costly. Some reputable hybrid companies charge between $10,000 and $45,000 to produce a book, others charge $250,000 or more for white-label services, with authors bearing the financial burden of production and marketing expenses. Quality and reputation can vary among hybrid publishers, so it's essential for authors to research and choose reputable companies. Additionally, authors may have less control over pricing and royalties compared to self-publishing. Despite these challenges, hybrid publishing offers a viable option for authors seeking a balance between creative control and professional support, and often with faster publishing processes.

SELF-PUBLISHING

Self-publishing refers to the process where an author independently publishes their work without the involvement of traditional or custom publishing houses. Authors retain full control over the content, cover design, pricing, and distribution channels. One major benefit is autonomy: Authors make all decisions and keep a higher percentage of royalties. Additionally, self-publishing allows for much faster publication, bypassing the lengthy traditional publishing process. It also offers access to a global audience through online platforms like Amazon Kindle Direct Publishing and IngramSpark.

However, self-publishing comes with challenges. Authors bear all expenses, including editing, cover design, and marketing. Without the support of traditional publishers, self-published books may struggle to gain recognition and distribution. Quality control can also be an issue, as some self-published works may lack professional editing or design. Moreover, authors must invest time and effort into marketing and promotion to reach their target audiences among a vast sea of self-published titles. Despite these drawbacks, self-publishing remains a viable option for authors seeking creative control and quicker access to readers.

TAKE ACTION

When it comes to publishing, there is no right answer—only what's right for your client. Build a list of companies you might consider recommending to clients, and create a list of pros and cons of each. Bonus points if you can find a contact at each company who can provide more information about their services and track record.

TRADITIONAL PUBLISHING:

Companies and literary agents you may consider working with:

_____

_____

_____

Pros + Cons:

_____

_____

_____

Contact:

_____

_____

_____

CUSTOM PUBLISHING:

Companies you may consider working with:

_____

_____

_____

Pros + Cons:

_____

_____

_____

Contact:

_____

_____

_____

SELF-PUBLISHING:

Companies you may consider working with:

_____

_____

_____

Pros + Cons:

_____

_____

_____

Contact:

_____

_____

_____

CHAPTER 11

Self-Promotion and Networking

When you pitch for a project, you want potential clients to find online evidence of your business when they ask about your services. That being said, your social media doesn't always have to be related to your bread-and-butter business. This is why having a professional website is important. Many professional writers also have a LinkedIn profile.

SETTING UP SOCIAL + WEBSITE

It is perfectly fine to hire someone to create your website, if it's within your budget and it has a well-thought-out design, or to create one yourself, if you know how. What you don't want is a poorly designed, slow-loading website that screams "Template!" with a cluttered layout, typos, and boring stock photos. Add some personality!

And be sure of one thing: The website you have now is not the website you will have for the rest of your career. It will evolve over time, just like you will as a writer.

Alice: How People Find Me

People most often find me through referrals, a Google search, or on platforms that connect authors and publishing professionals, and then they check me out on LinkedIn. At that point, they will likely find my personal website and message me there. I have over 6,500 connections on LinkedIn, but I don't post as often as others do. Even though I don't use the platform as effectively as some, it serves as a valid placeholder that shows people I am a legitimate writer with online articles to read and a nice-looking website.

Alee: The Power of Podcasts

I market to my niche through guest appearances on podcasts. I've also been in and around the grief community in Nashville, so I'm known in that realm. Even when I lead a grief meeting or group, I'm networking (though not purposefully) simply because I'm interacting and associating with like-minded people. Recently, clients have come to me and said, "When I found you, I listened to all of your podcasts, and I really enjoyed what you had to say," or, "I feel like I already know you because I've listened to your podcasts." I also pay for Google Ads and have found them incredibly helpful in generating leads!

NETWORKING AND REFERRALS

When we talk about networking, we're referring to two different types: one is networking outside the writing and publishing industry to connect with those in need of your services. This means if your niche is writing about health and wellness, get in front of personal trainers, nutritionists, or sports scientists. Go to their conferences. Join their online Facebook groups. Connect with them on LinkedIn. Build relationships wherever you can. The other is networking within the industry with people like writers, editors, literary agents, publishers, and designers. These are the people you'll get referrals from, refer to, or hire for editorial work.

When it comes to networking and marketing, pay attention to what your peers are doing. If you see on social media that everyone is joining a masterclass or someone you admire is attending an event in your area, consider joining those. Do the things that others do, as long as you'll genuinely enjoy the experience. Observe the actions of those within your niche or community who are ahead of you or whose careers you wish to emulate, and mimic what they are doing.

Both of us have spoken on panels about writing and publishing. Panels are a great way to establish yourself as an expert and to add your voice to the mix. We've also taught several writing classes and workshops and taken writing classes to learn new perspectives and skills. There's always more to learn about writing.

It's important to give back to the writing and publishing community when you can with time, expertise, and money. For instance, if someone refers a client to you, you should plan to pay them around 5-10% of your fee as a token of your appreciation—they may even ask for it. Industry-wide, 5% is the norm for referral fees. However, if someone has invested a lot of time nurturing that relationship, it is not uncommon for them to ask for 10%.

Send those fees as a thank-you without hesitation, because you want the person to be excited to receive surprise "mailbox money," as our friend and mentor Honorée Corder calls it. You want them to remain your advocate, and you can bet they will if you take care of them.

If you're pitched a project you don't want or can't take on, especially as you grow and niche down, you will be the one referring projects to others someday. Think of it as paying your dues and adding some insurance to your business relationships.

MENTORSHIP SESSIONS

Do not be afraid to ask writers you admire for mentorship sessions. In those sessions, get comfortable with being vulnerable. Ask the questions you really need the answers to, and stay open to receiving that information. Someone might tell you when they think you're charging too little, but they'll also tell you if they believe you're charging too much for your services at your current experience level.

Also, just as with referrals, think about how you can compensate them for their time, even if they don't ask you for money (which they might!). Whether you send them a gift card, a small gift, or buy them a cup of coffee, make sure they know you are grateful and recognize their time and support.

NETWORKING DOS AND DONT'S: THE ART OF HAVING GOOD CONVERSATIONS WITH TOTAL STRANGERS

So, what if you want to go to networking events but you're nervous? Join the club! The first few years of trying to network as a freelancer are all about learning how to have productive conversations—how to ask open-ended questions and how to talk about yourself and your career in a way that makes people want to ask more questions.

Through trial, error, and standing awkwardly in the corner (looking at you, Alice), we've learned some networking lessons that guarantee the best experience for the time and effort we expend.

Lesson 1: Attend fewer, more targeted networking events.

While this may initially seem counterintuitive, the concept of quality over quantity applies here. We'd rather you attend five networking events a year that pertain to writing, publishing, or a related topic than 215 events just because they're local.

Lesson 2: Bring a guest, or make sure you know someone at each event you attend.

We know we keep talking about it, but relationships are important. Get one of your friends or colleagues to go with you as a social buffer if you're shy, or to compare notes with and maximize your networking potential if you're more extroverted. There's safety—and bravery—in numbers.

You can also practice bragging about your friend to people you meet, with the understanding that they'll return the favor. It's often far easier to gush about your friends and their accomplishments than your own., so let your friends do the same for you—and then, you can leave at the same time, so you're not stuck there alone.

Lesson 3: Choose events that energize, educate, and inspire you.

We've attended industry-related events packed with publishers, writers, editors, and designers, but they were so uninspiring and disorganized that we never went back. On the other hand, we've been to events that left us feeling fulfilled and energized beyond expectations because they aligned with our interests, skill sets, and values. Listen to your gut and choose wisely.

Lesson 4: Network online with intention.

You might enjoy smaller, more intentional venues where networking comes a little easier, both online and in person. There are plenty of social media groups and literary organizations where you can connect with other writers, editors, and creatives, such as the Authors Guild (see Resources for more specifics).

You can also find writer meetup groups and workshops in random coffee shops or community spaces almost anywhere. There are plenty of online writing groups, and if you don't find one that feels quite right, you can start your own!

Because being a writer is largely a solo act, we cannot emphasize enough the importance of carving out your own community—not only so you make connections and get paid, but to also maintain your sanity. There are countless resources on social media, with tons of groups and communities where writers can bond over their writing, swap stories, and ask for advice. It's important to remember that community is networking, and networking is community.

Writing conferences can be great, because they're usually well-attended, allowing you to connect with others in the industry. The opportunity to learn more about your craft is irreplaceable. Conferences can be expensive and often involve travel, but they can be amazing networking experiences.

Workshops, whether in person or online, can also be great spaces to learn more about a particular topic. Although workshops often have a much smaller number of participants, there's a greater opportunity to be seen and heard in a way you might not be at a large conference. Again, this is a smart way to make connections and get answers to questions you have about specific topics.

If you have just graduated or left your job and have tons of time and energy to network, do it—but also pay attention to what you like and what you don't. Being intentional in all aspects of our lives can only be a positive.

THE MENTOR/MENTEE UNDERSTANDING AND RELATIONSHIP

We've already mentioned the great benefits of finding a mentor and building a relationship with someone who is further long in their journey. However, we have some additional advice to offer you while we're on this topic.

If you find somebody open to having a mentoring conversation, that's amazing. And, yes, it's certainly okay to ask someone you admire or want to emulate to meet for coffee or lunch or to jump on a 15-minute call. They may agree to food or drink as payment for their time and expertise, but you also need to be prepared for responses like, "Sure, here's my link—this is what it costs for a consulting session." And you shouldn't be offended by it. You're going to be running a business just like the writers you're reaching out to—and no one is obligated to do anything for free. Our time is our most valuable commodity, along with our expertise, and we should be compensated for sharing with others.

TAKE ACTION

Try Your Hand at Networking

Now that you have your elevator pitch and a sense of what networking as a freelancer looks like, it's time to give it a go. Your assignment, should you choose to accept it, is to:

- Research local networking events.

- Reach out to friends who may be good event buddies.

- Go to one event this month and hand out five business cards (if you have them) to people with whom you've made a personal connection.

- Try out your elevator pitch.

Remember, you aren't aiming for perfection or to leave each event with ten new clients. You're just trying to put yourself out there. Remember, it's a process. Every time you meet a new person is a chance to expand your network and sharpen your pitch. You never know which conversation will lead to a new project down the line.

CHAPTER 12

Your First Leads

So, how do ghostwriters get work? At this point, it hopefully won't surprise you to hear that the secret is relationships (with a little hustle on the side). You have to connect with people and keep those connections going—and when you get a chance, you go all in, making sure you're doing good work and getting it done on time.

We both worked in publishing while moonlighting for other book agencies, so we did know some people in the industry when we took the leap. But we also still nurture those relationships to this day. You know why? Because, other than delivering on what we claim we can do, connections are the most important part of growing our businesses.

If you're interested in writing nonfiction, you can, of course, work with private clients. You can also connect with literary agencies, publishing houses of all types (traditional, custom/hybrid, and more), law firms that focus on entertainment or intellectual property (IP), magazines, newspapers, blogs, and any other organization that regularly releases written content. Once you start letting people know who you are and what you can do for them, you'll find leads everywhere.

Alee: On The Power of Making Connections

When I got laid off from HarperCollins, I handed out more than 100 resumes to colleagues—via email, in the halls, literally everywhere I could think of. Then, I thought back to my college internship at MTV, a fashion PR company in NYC where my life became a living hell, and even a few companies where I did temp work. I thought about every personal and professional connection I'd ever made and began to formulate a plan.

By the time my last day came, I had a handwritten list of about 150 people on my desk. I made it my mission to reconnect with ten of them each week until I'd contacted everyone. Not all of them responded—not even close—and I didn't land 150 book deals, either. But I did get a ton of leads, and several of those leads became clients—and those clients paid me to write!

Alice: Persistence Pays Off

To make my earliest connections, I went to so many networking events, even if they weren't industry-related: tech, singles, women in business, and whatever other categories I could find. I also called all of my past gigs, no matter how long I was there— the sports desk at the Tennessean; my post-college Country Music Television (CMT) internship; a pub house (I was there six weeks); and Thomas Nelson, where I worked for years. I even co-taught several semesters of a writing workshop at my church, which, amazingly, resulted in 13 published books.

I knew I needed to keep in touch with all those people, so I became an annoying fly. I would email everyone once every few weeks, reminding them of my availability and following up on any previous conversations we'd had. It was a brilliant and effective strategy.

When I was the managing editor for my division at the publishing house, I always had a list of between 12-20 vetted freelancers. And you know which ones I chose for each project? The ones who reached out to tell me they had availability. Their persistence made the choice easy for me, and they benefited financially.

Even today, my relationships are still a significant part of my business. Of my last 45 clients (ghostwriting books, ghostwriting book proposals, and doing developmental reviews), here's how we connected:

- *19 people found me through an online search.*

- *10 were referrals from other industry people.*

- *13 were through a literary matchmaking agency.*

- *3 were people I met at networking events.*

As you start out, make and keep your connections, reach outside your comfort zone, and be creative about it. Everybody uses words, and there are a million ways you can pitch yourself. Network. And use your connections wisely.

MAKING (AND KEEPING) CONNECTIONS

Networking is most valuable when you make it meaningful. And by that, we don't just mean making a connection—it's about remembering the conversations you have with individuals and recalling those details in future communications. Your goal is to build genuine relationships, not to be just another email in someone's inbox.

For example, if you do contract work for a literary agency, get to know everyone who works there on a personal level. Schedule a 15-minute call with the editor, the project manager, and anyone else you can, including the agency's owner. Often, you can easily find these contacts by looking at who is listed on the agency's website.

People are more willing to respond (and send work your way) when they feel like they know you. When they know you—and especially when they know your work—they'll advocate for you within the company. You might not have a lot of coworkers in this profession, but if you create genuine relationships with people, those bonds will be helpful for both your morale and your workload.

FIRST PHONE CALLS

We want to highlight something before we get into specifics of that first phone call with a potential client. Both of us are introverts who don't love putting ourselves out there. We've mentioned our shyness, but it might be easy to read all this and think, *Okay, but they're better with people than I am*, or, *This is too hard for me*, or, *I'll probably die of over-socialization*. Many writers are more introverted, partly because of the solitary nature of the work. However, if you want to be a professional writer who isn't stuck in the feast-or-famine cycle, you're going to have to fake it. Pretend. Be a character. Be someone else for a hot minute.

Alee pretends to be one of her friends when she's networking. Alice has a character, too—a sassy librarian. If you're shy, introverted, or awkward and want to take a stab at this, you'll have to make networking work for you—and we know you will. Plus, it does get easier as you take on more projects and gain more practice talking to complete strangers.

And here's the thing: First phone calls with potential clients can feel scary. Your mindset in these moments is everything. Keep it simple, stay clear, and remind yourself before the call even begins that you are not the only one being interviewed here. You are also interviewing them! Pay attention to your gut feelings from the get-go.

You can start initial calls by introducing yourself and asking how their day is going, where they're located, and how the weather is. We know, it sounds cliché, but small talk helps put the potential client at ease. Then, you can say, "Tell me a bit more about your project and your goals," to get the dialogue flowing. From there, build off what they say, and **don't hesitate to ask clarifying questions**.

Great follow-up questions include, "What books do you like?" or "What books are similar to what you want to write?" If they've mentioned their publishing goals, ask for more details. For example, if they say they want to be traditionally published as opposed to self-published, ask what type of publisher they're aiming for and if they know their social media numbers. Some may be shooting for the moon, while others might just want to see their name in print.

You can also ask about their ideal audience and readership, their reasons for writing (both personally and professionally) and if they have a specific timeline in mind for completing the project. It's always smart to ask if they already have written material or content they want to include in the book (especially for memoirs), whether there are other people you'll need to interview for the book, and how much research they think will be involved. All these questions give you a better understanding of projects you may collaborate on and will help you generate may be collaborating on and help you generate a quote.

If at any point you start to get the feeling that you're not a good fit for a person or their project—whether it's because you get a bad vibe from the call or the book is about a topic you greatly dislike or have no interest in—it's perfectly okay to say, "Thank you for considering me, but I don't think I'm a good fit for this project." Also, you don't have to stay on a call if someone makes you uncomfortable. Remember, this is your show, and you run it.

Ask if they have questions about you and your process, and if they don't, give them a brief overview anyway. We always ask—*always*—"Have you spoken to other writers? Have they told you what their process is?" Whether they have or not, remind them most writers work differently, and then give an overview of *your* approach, explaining why you've found it to be the most effective way to work—more details on this soon!

This means, by the way, that you need to have at least an outline of your process written down before you get on your first call. We're going to give you some starter templates, and while you may not have every detail figured out, you need to have a plan. You might even want to practice parts of this conversation in front of a mirror or with friends before you have it.

This is especially true for your very first book. You're not faking your talent—you know you can do this for them. However, you shouldn't get on the call and say, "Hey, I'm a ghostwriting virgin. Money, please!" You want to frame the conversation in a way that shows you know what you're doing, even if you're internally freaking out. Show up with a clear process, a thoughtful approach to their topic, and demonstrate a genuine love of storytelling. All these things will make a good impression. You need to exude confidence, because if you allow yourself to be an anxious wreck, they'll pick up on it—and you *do* know what you're doing, even if you're nervous.

You might ask: *Are you telling me to lie about my work experience?*

No. Don't lie and say you've written ten books when you haven't written your first one yet. Honesty paired with enthusiasm is always the best approach.

This can be an awkward conversation, but it doesn't have to be. Make a list of all the reasons you love writing, reading, and storytelling, and work those into the conversation. Talk about your favorite authors, why you love them, and what makes their writing unique in your opinion. If you have any previous writing experience, be sure to mention that as well. (Remember that, at this stage, you should have several writing samples, even if you had to create them specifically for this purpose.)

If someone asks whether you've written a book before and you haven't, you can honestly say that while this may be your first full-length project, you have a process and a timeline to follow, you're a great listener and a hard worker, and you're looking forward to helping them write their book. You could also say something like this, tailored to your own experience: "I've written multiple articles / white papers / speeches / etc., and I'm excited to use my skills on a lengthier project."

SET REALISTIC TIMELINES

Speaking of timelines, don't fall into the trap of giving yourself exactly enough time to complete a project. Exactly enough is not enough. For instance, we both typically allot six to ten months to complete a memoir. The first month is for interviews, the next four to six are for drafting, and the final months are for edits. Are all of our projects always wrapped up in exactly six months? Nope. Some are shorter, while others are way longer.

Alee just finished a book in two months, but she has others that take close to a year. Alice once wrote a book in twenty-one days, but ended up with strep and the flu from not sleeping. (We do not recommend accepting such ridiculous and rushed timelines.) Life happens, and clients have different needs, so keep timelines reasonable. Let potential clients know that you'll keep communication open and remain flexible. If a client absolutely needs a book completed in a short period, you can add a rush fee into your contract.

Your timelines are personal to you, and much of it will depend on your workload and your client's availability. If you have four clients, writing a full-length book in three months is probably not realistic. If you have one or two clients, you might be all right. Take stock and always be evaluating. Just remember: Potential clients don't need to know the specifics of your workload. Don't feel pressured to disclose exactly how many projects you're tackling at once. Instead, use that knowledge to generate a realistic delivery date on your end.

When people ask you outright how many projects you work on at a time (and some will ask), you can tell them you typically handle two or three simultaneously. You can explain that all these projects are at different stages and cover different topics, which helps keep your creative process sharp.

It's also important not to overpromise and underdeliver. If you can't take on another project, it's okay to say so and to ask if you can begin the work in a few months instead. If they want to start the project now, take it as your chance to get your first referral fee by connecting them with another writer who has immediate availability.

You'll eventually have someone say they want to be your only client. At first, you might be tempted to agree and turn away other work, but be cautious—they might be less concerned about your attention to the project and more concerned about your attention to them personally. Some clients want to be able to call at all hours of the day and night and get an immediate response.

In that situation, you can say, "I would be happy for you to be my only client if you're willing to pay $5,000 / $15,000 / $30,000 a month." That number will change as your experience increases—and even if they are your only client, they must still respect your boundaries.

MONEY TALK

Money conversations can be some of the most awkward, but they're also the most important! Whenever possible, avoid having these discussions face-to-face. It's far too easy to agree to less money if a potential client asks for a discount or shares a personal story that tugs at your heartstrings. We've both had calls where we felt confident at the start, but by the end, we'd lowered our rates by half because we felt bad for the client. And guess what? We created a whole bunch of unnecessary frustration and resentment by saying yes when we should have held our ground—but we still had to do the work with excellence, knowing that we caved.

At the start of your career, you might be more flexible with pricing. You can consider the potential client's budget against your financial needs and time, especially as you're trying to build experience. Whatever you choose, we've found that it works well to indicate pricing early on.

After all, you can spend hours nurturing "potential clients" through calls and emails only to find out they can't afford your services. That's why we suggest getting the pricing conversation out of the way via email in advance of a call. The goal is that by the time you're on your initial call, everyone understands the money situation or at least has a clear idea of the range. That way, if a potential client backs out once they hear your pricing, it's okay!

This is a business, so money talk is inevitable. Perhaps this part is where you thrive, and you can't wait to stand firm on your pricing. Maybe you're terrified and would rather hide in a closet. Regardless, face it head-on and hold your ground. Be discerning and watch for potential hiccups. And remember, if the project isn't a good fit for you for any reason, you can always refer it to another writer and ask for a referral fee.

Referral fees are a standard practice in many industries, including writing. If you pass along a warm lead to another writer, you can ask for a 5-10% referral fee if they move forward with the project. Likewise, you should be thrilled to pay a referral fee to another writer if they pass work onto you, because you didn't have to do any marketing to get the lead.

It's important to note that when people in a corporate structure recommend you, they might be stuck in a static, scarcity mindset and expect you to be willing to undercut your prices to get work. We both experienced this as a result of past work in publishing houses where budgets were tight. Remember, you are providing a service worth money, and you're not being high-maintenance by asking clients to honor that.

Once you've shared your prices, the potential client usually will usually respond in one of three ways:

1. That's out of my budget, but if something changes, I'll get back with you.

3. If you can send me the details, I'll think about it/talk it over with a business partner/spouse/other advisor and get back to you in a few days.

4. Sounds great! Send the contract over, and we'll get started.

TAKE ACTION

Write a Script for Your First Client Call

Draft a script for your first potential client call. You won't need to follow it word for word, but having it in front of you can help boost your confidence, and you can refer to it if you get nervous. Remember to discuss the following topics:

- Your process, your experience, and potentially your favorite books or authors

- Their reason for writing the book (personal, professional or both)

- Their goals and expectations for the book

- Their intended audience

- Any thoughts on publishing paths (traditional, hybrid, self)

- What work they've already done (research, written notes, outlines)

- Industry standard sizing (either in word count, page count, or trim size) for the genre of book they wish to write

If they ask about money, remember to say you'll provide a quote within 48 hours of the call once you've been able to review all factors.

Once you've drafted your script, say it aloud, and practice it with a friend or fellow writer. Notice if anything feels clunky or unnatural. Adjust your script until it feels like you.

Bonus Script for Referral Fees

If you want to pass a project to another writer and would like a referral fee, you can email them something like this:

"Hey there! I've been contacted by an author with a great project, but [it's not a great fit for me, or I don't have the availability, and] I would like to send them your way. I'd like to ask for a [5-10% referral fee], and if that's okay with you, I'll be happy to make the connection!"

Keep in mind that unless you ask another writer to sign an agreement honoring your referral fee arrangement, which some writers do, it's largely an honor system. If you send another writer a project and they forget to send you the referral fee you asked for, it's okay to check in and ask how the project is going to gently nudge them. If they still don't send you the agreed-upon fee, send your future referrals to someone else.

CHAPTER 13

Negotiating Contracts

Here we are, at the most exciting and critical stage of our onboarding process. This is the moment when everything becomes real—the time when it's critical not only to know your worth but to define how you want to complete it. In general, ghostwriters should use contracts to establish clear expectations, scope of work, timeline, and payment terms. Contracts protect ghostwriters by outlining project details, deadlines, and payment schedules, and offering legal recourse if things go south and you need to resolve any disputes. We know this time can be thrilling, but it can also be incredibly overwhelming. Don't worry—we've got you covered!

BUILDING YOUR BASE CONTRACT

The vast majority of ghostwriters are not lawyers, so we need to find ways to protect ourselves by using services or consulting with professionals to get the ball rolling. Ideally, you would hire a literary or entertainment lawyer to build your base contract, which you can customize as needed. If budget is a concern (as it often is when you're just starting out), websites like LegalZoom are great options. You might also consider checking Fiverr or Upwork for an affordable lawyer to consult with. It's also an option to combine the two—generate a contract using LegalZoom and hire an affordable attorney on Fiverr or Upwork to review it.

WHAT TO INCLUDE IN YOUR CONTRACT

As with most things, the more experience you have with clients, the more you'll discover specific line items that need to be added to your contract. To save you from some of our own hard-knock lessons, we've found the following items helpful to include in your base contract:

- **Working Hours and Communication** – These are essentially your in-office hours, indicating when you're available to respond to emails and calls. This doesn't *need* to be 9–5 every weekday. It can be whatever schedule works best for you. You'll also need to decide whether you'll record all work-related calls or only certain ones. (We suggest recording all of them post-contract signing and letting clients know ahead of time.)

- **Holidays** – This section should state that you observe all federal holidays, include any personal holidays, and outline your time-off procedures. (For example, specify whether you'll respond to texts or calls during these breaks.)

- **Mode of Communication** – Clearly specify whether the client should contact you via email, text, or phone call. You may even choose to use platforms like WhatsApp, Voxer, Signal, or another chat service to keep client communication separate from your personal life. Some writers have a separate work number they share with clients.

- **Plagiarism** – If the client provides content that is plagiarized, you're not responsible for their errors. (However, I do strongly recommend running all client content through a plagiarism checker like Grammarly—it can save your butt!)

- **AI** – With the rise of programs like ChatGPT, it's important to clearly state that you will not use AI in the creation of content.

If the client has used AI in the creation of their initial content, you'll need to know what it is and completely rewrite it.

- **Client Responsibility** – Outline the client's responsibilities, including timely communication, the need to purchase and become familiar with Microsoft Word (especially Track Changes), and their availability for interviews.

- **Payment Schedule** – Always ask for at least a 10% down payment on signing. After that, you can either set up monthly payments (which we both recommend) or agree to receive payments upon the delivery of pages or specific word count goals (as an example: chapter outline and first chapter / 25,000 words / 50,000 words / completion).

- **Travel** – If you're required to travel for in-person meetings, you can choose to do so at the client's expense, asking them to cover or reimburse costs like flights, hotels, and car rentals if needed. In some cases, you can also charge a per diem based on your state's rates.[2]

We have also added a clause stating that if 30 days passes without any contact from the client, the contract is null and void. This was necessary after having several experiences where we sent the first draft or round of edits and then did not hear from the client for half a year or more. One person went dark for well over a year and then popped up, expecting to resume work immediately, causing Alice to shuffle her schedule around.

Another helpful clause to have in your contract is one that states that you, as the contractor, own the copyright for the work until the contract has been paid in full. Again, we've had several instances where a client skipped out on the final payment and published the book anyway.

---

[2] Visit https://www.gsa.gov/travel/plan-book/per-diem-rates for your state's rates.

So, lawyer up if you can. Get a foundational contract in place and keep your lawyer on hand for the inevitable times you'll need them again. Your contract will evolve over time based on your needs, your clientele, and even your genre. All of this is okay—just make sure you're prepared for it.

We understand it might sound intimidating to hear us suggest getting a lawyer, but we promise you, it's quite the opposite. When dealing with any kind of art, remember that nearly everything is subjective. This means things can sometimes get messy. That's why it's important to have someone qualified who will have your back.

HONOR CONTRACT TERMS (AND KNOW WHEN TO REVISE)

When you send off the initial contract for a project, we know you'll do your very best to estimate time, effort, and scope accurately. While most of the time things will go as expected, there will be times when they don't. Contracts might end early, but more often, they'll need to be extended. What happens when you agree to write up to 60,000 words, but the manuscript ends up pushing 80,000? That's considered "scope creep," and you need a clause in your contract to address it, but you also need to feel comfortable bringing it up with the client. A contract clause does no good if you don't enforce it.

> ### *Alice: Scope Creep*
>
> *I once had a project that wildly diverged from what we originally anticipated. When I noticed that the scope of the project was no longer accurate, I scheduled a conversation and said, "At the rate we're going, I feel confident in saying this project is not going to be 60,000 words—it very well could be 200,000 words. If that's the case, the options are: a) revise the scope of the contract and renegotiate the amount, or b) keep it to our agreed-*

upon word count, which will mean cutting a lot of material, and you'll need to stop sending me new content to be added."

This is a prime example of setting an important boundary so you don't get taken advantage of. While most clients won't intentionally exploit you, I have yet to meet one who has realized the scope has changed and has offered to send me the extra $20,000 out of the kindness of their hearts.

Another situation that can change the scope of a contract is the need to pause for one reason or another—whether it's financial, medical, or some other life circumstance. During the pandemic, a client and her partner both got COVID, so we had to pause the project for five months.

Another time, I had a different client change his mind about the type of book he wanted to write after I had already written the entire first draft. He'd paid me in advance via cashier's checks to hold his space on my calendar. Although he wasn't ready to begin the revision process, he told me to keep cashing the checks each month and said, "I'll get around to the new book eventually."

While I loved the guaranteed money at the time, two years later, when he resumed the contract, the project had become a completely different, longer book with four additional authors. Since I had already been paid for the work according to the original contract but "the work" had changed significantly, it felt like I was then working for free.

This is yet another case for revising the contract and setting clear boundaries, my friends.

Signature Time!

Once the contract is complete and all terms have been agreed upon, it's time to sign. While it's preferred to use a service like DocuSign, you can also have the client simply sign a PDF electronically, or print a Word document for them to sign and send back to you. However you do it, have the client sign first, then you sign second. Then, send a scan of a "fully executed copy" (a copy with both signatures) to the client and store another copy securely for your records. We recommend utilizing a cloud storage service for saving these important documents. Saving them locally on your desktop and risking a computer crash or theft, which could result in losing all of your contracts, is asking for trouble. Trust us.

HOLD CLIENTS ACCOUNTABLE

While a lot of the pressure is on you, as the writer, to deliver, every book is a collaborative partnership, and your clients are accountable for their part of the deal. This issue crops up most often in one of three areas: turnarounds, payment, and ghosting (the vanishing type, not the writing type).

For turnarounds, set clear expectations early on about how quickly they need to return edits or changes to you. We typically give clients two weeks and ask them to follow up with us if it's going to go beyond that. We also set a date to check in with them at the one-week mark. If we reach the two-week deadline and they haven't submitted, we send an email reminding them of the due date. If we hear nothing within a week, we continue to follow up every couple of days—but we stop working until we receive their feedback.

If a client is late paying your invoice, it can be especially awkward when you are first starting out. Remember: You delivered the work and deserve to be paid on time. Send a friendly reminder on the due date, then follow up weekly. Don't worry about coming across as pushy; this isn't just about the money, it's about maintaining professional boundaries that respect your time and work.

For clients who are consistently late, consider requesting upfront payment for future projects (if you choose to continue working with them). And in the rare circumstance when you get ghosted by a client, you can have your lawyer send a letter requesting the payment you are due. It's amazing how quickly you'll get paid once a lawyer is involved.

HOW TO SPOT A PREDATOR (OR JUST A BAD DEAL)

While we'd love nothing more than to focus solely on all the positive aspects of ghostwriting, that wouldn't be realistic. We want you to know how to spot a predator, whether a private client or a company, because they do exist. We'll dive into client red flags in Chapter 20, but as you are thinking about projects, proposals, and your first leads, we want you to be prepared.

AGENCIES

If an agency lets you set your price, your payment schedule, and pays you as soon as you've completed the work, they're probably safe to do business with. However, some agencies may ignore your desired pricing and have a one-size-fits-all model. They'll set their price and pay you a percentage of what the author is paying them—usually 30% or less for doing 90% of the work. We're not saying you should shut the deal down altogether, since these can be good options for first-time writers, but there are intricacies you should understand before you enter into this type of negotiation. The first and most obvious is that you'll likely be getting paid much less money than what you could charge on your own with a private client.

And even though you always give 100% effort to every project you take on, the time and attention you dedicate to each one won't always align with the compensation you receive. Additionally, some agencies might say they'll pay you "once the client has given feedback" without providing a set pay schedule or turnaround timeline. This dynamic only hurts you, not the agency, so think twice in these situations. Read the contract carefully, negotiate terms, and be aware of the potential pitfalls, especially as you become more established.

ROYALTIES

As you dive into this business and start talking to prospective clients, you'll find that some will try to hire you while lowering or completely eliminating your fee by offering you a percentage of their sales on the back end of a project, also known as royalties. However, as industry insiders, we know this is usually a bad deal, although there are always exceptions. (We know a ghost who agreed to write a short proposal for no money up front but a large percentage of a potential publishing advance, which netted her several hundred thousand dollars when the client got a huge book deal.) A royalty, a mention on the cover, or even an acknowledgement should be an enticement or an added bonus—it should rarely, if ever, replace your rate.

The truth is, books are just as hard to market and sell as they are to write, and the process is entirely out of your hands. While it is ultimately your choice, stay aware and remember to assert your worth.

What you need to understand about book publishing is that if somebody goes with a mainstream, traditional publisher, they are given an advance, but it is not a payment, as most people assume—it's debt. Before the author earns a single additional penny in royalties, the publisher recoups the entire advance through sales. So, when you're offered royalties as compensation, remember that the chance of earning anything substantial is very low. Unless it's a sure thing (which is super rare and almost nonexistent), you're signing up for a huge risk that's unlikely to work out in your favor.

Most of the time, you're going to invest 300–500 hours of work into a book that the author may not even decide to publish—which, by the way, you have no control over. Even if they do publish the book, you're dependent on them to market it, sell books, and send you quarterly payments and royalties. It's a hassle. That said, Alice does have one author who still sends her royalties twice a year to this day. It's always a sweet surprise to receive unexpected mailbox money, but you can't count on that as guaranteed or significant income.

If you're looking for a sign that someone may bring up royalties, take note if they mention personal financial struggles or try to guilt you somehow in early conversations. Be prepared for it. This isn't to say you can't be empathetic, but remember that you're in this business primarily to make money. Guilt trips will happen, but you have no obligation to lower your fee based on someone's circumstances.

Alice: Just Say No to Aloha

It's entirely possible you'll encounter a situation where you believe royalties might pay off. Just never forget to consider your circumstances and trust your gut. You might have plenty of savings, or you could be one paycheck away from being financially strapped—these are two completely different scenarios. Also, keep in mind that if you agree to a royalties-only arrangement, you're still committed to doing the work, even if you become resentful during the process.

For example, early in my career, I agreed to work for a royalties-only publishing company based in Hawaii. In addition to helping with the writing and editing, it was also my job to help market the book—and I had zero experience with marketing. I said yes for two reasons: I had no idea what I was agreeing to, and, honestly, I thought it was pretty cool in my twenties to say I worked for a publishing company out of Hawaii!

I did all the work, and the author only sold ten copies a year. Once or twice a year, over the lifetime of the project, I'd get a PayPal notification saying, "Aloha, enclosed is your payment for $0.96." I think I made less than $20 over the entire course of the project. Not nearly as cool as I thought, in retrospect.

WORKING WITH COUPLES

All relationships can be complicated, but the ghostwriter-couple relationship can be particularly so. While working with couples isn't inherently a red flag, it's important to recognize that you're managing more than just one interpersonal dynamic. While both of us have successfully worked with couples, it's important to be aware that the addition of another active (or passive) participant can significantly change the dynamics.

Alee: I'm Not a Couples Counselor

I once worked with a couple who could not get on the same page. The wife would approve content and then weeks later, once I had already written more, the husband would come back and reject the whole thing. The process was clunky throughout, and ultimately, neither husband nor wife was 100% happy with the end product. The last straw was a Zoom call where the couple started fighting while I sat there biting my nails. Right then, I promised never to work with another couple. It just wasn't worth the headache.

Alice: Going Undercover

I once wrote a fiction book with an author who had a complicated couple dynamic. The author had previously been the breadwinner but was now staying home to raise the kids. When we worked together, she was on a tight budget set by her husband. She didn't want him to know what she was paying me out of her monthly allowance, so sometimes she would meet me at a restaurant and hand me an envelope full of cash. It was weird.

Another time, I was working with someone who enjoyed our work together, but his wife did not because she wanted to write her own book. Partway through the project, the wife—not my client—fired me. I don't think he ever finished his book.

TAKE ACTION

Phone Call FAQ

Negotiation calls can be intense, and it's easy to get thrown off by client questions and comments. We've compiled a list of common WTF phone moments and potential answers you can keep handy, just in case your clients are like ours (i.e., human).

Client Statement 1: This is going to be the next *New York Times* Bestseller / Pulitzer Prize-winning novel / sell a million copies. It'll be a great career move for you, so you should lower your fee accordingly (or even work for free because of the exposure you'll receive by being connected to this amazing project)!

Response*: I really hope that's true, and I'm excited about the potential. However, I do want to set realistic expectations. Those are very high goals, and while I will do everything in my power to make that happen, we may need to adjust our targets as we progress. Additionally, there are many factors outside of my control when it comes to achieving sales of this magnitude, so I must stick to my full fee.*

Client Statement 2: You'll learn a lot from me. That should be taken into account with your fee.

Response: *While I'm excited about the opportunity to exchange knowledge, I don't discount my services based on that. The exchange of ideas is valuable, but my fee reflects the work and expertise I bring to the project.*

Client Statement 3: I have tons of journal entries, so I should receive a discount for words already written.

Response: *While I appreciate the material you're bringing to the table, we'll primarily use it for context. The effort required on my part to craft the final manuscript remains the same, so this won't result in a reduced fee.*

Client Statement 4: I have three kids in college, so I can't afford your services. Will you give me a steep discount?

Response: *Unfortunately, my rates are firm. However, I'm happy to suggest another writer who might fit within your budget.*

Client Statement 5: I am a Christian / pastor doing the Lord's work. You should lower your fee.

Response: *Though I appreciate the work you're doing, that doesn't affect my rate. My fee remains the same.*

CHAPTER 14

Kicking Off Your First Project

All terms are agreed upon, the contract is signed, and now it's time to get to work! Your first order of business is to schedule a kickoff call with the client to get the ball rolling. In general, the goal of your first few calls is to nail down what exactly the book is about. And when we say *exactly*, we mean just that. Your goal is to come to an agreement on the book's overview (a high-level summary), key takeaways, and audience profile. These elements are crucial for fully understanding the client's vision.

To make things easier, before your first call, you can send the client a form to fill out with the following questions (sometimes, they'll have already discussed some of the answers with you on your earlier get-to-know-you call):

- In two sentences, describe your book's content.
- What is your purpose for writing the book?
- What genre do you consider your book to be?
- What are the primary themes of the book?
- What is the book's tone?
- Who is your target audience?
- Write a preliminary outline (bullet points of what you'd like the book to include).

Most of the time, a client will fill out this form themselves, but sometimes they'll ask for help. Either way, this gives you a great jumping-off point for your first call.

GETTING THE MOST OUT OF INITIAL CALLS

Your very first goal is to create a robust overview, key takeaways, audience profile, and a chapter outline for the client. The best part is that the vast majority of this work can be accomplished during these initial calls. The number of calls, frequency, and overall hours required will vary with each project, but for example, Alice aims to have 12-15 hours of calls scheduled in the first 4-6 weeks. She schedules them 2-3 times a week, 60-90 minutes each. Additional calls are scheduled once she's drafting the chapters and needs even more granular details. A full book project might require between 40-80 hours of interview time overall.

Take copious notes on the client's ideas for the overview, and record all client calls! If you're a quick writer and can think on your feet, try typing out a few sentences to read aloud to the client, such as: "A gripping memoir about overcoming, [[title]] is a book that promises great storytelling and lessons learned from a lifetime in the shadow of an abusive parent."

To help the client provide some substantial key takeaways, ask the following questions:

- How do you want your reader to feel and think after reading your book?

- If the reader could only learn one thing from the book, what would it be?

- What action(s) do you want them to take after reading your book?

To build your audience profile, ask:

- Who is your ideal reader? ("Everyone" is not an acceptable or accurate answer.)

To begin your outline, ask these questions and take notes in bullet form:

- When does your story begin?
- Give me a high-level overview of the most important plot points.
- Are there certain events you'd like to include?
- Tell me your story **briefly**.

Once you have all this material, spend some time expanding and refining it. Write the overview like it is going to become the back cover copy, so the client can see the real potential. Finesse the outline as best you can, but keep in mind that it will likely need revisions. The final step is sending it out for approval!

BUILDING YOUR OUTLINE

Creating a book outline is a crucial step. It's your time to transform your client's scattered ideas into a cohesive roadmap for the manuscript you'll build. Start by critically looking at your overview and identifying the book's central theme or message, then break your notes into major sections or chapters that support this core concept. For personal development books, consider using a logical progression: chronological, problem-to-solution, or general-to-specific. For memoir, you'll want it to be chronological; you're typically not covering the author's whole life, just a period in their life.

Outline key plot points, character arcs, and major scenes. Don't aim for perfection initially; instead, create a flexible framework that captures your main ideas and their relationships. You can use simple bullet points or specialized software like Scrivener, but be sure to choose a method that feels right for you. Remember that your outline is a living document that will evolve as you write, serving as both a guide to keep you on track and a reference to ensure your book maintains focus and momentum from start to finish. Having it approved by the client is also the best way to make sure that you agree about what's going in the book from the start.

CREATING PROCESSES AND TEMPLATES

So, you've finished your first few phone calls, and your outline and overview are complete and approved—now, it's time to dive into the meat of your work.

As you tackle your first project, in addition to getting the work done, focus on creating your process and templates for all future projects. You'll have plenty of time to fine-tune as you go, so start project one with the intention of building something you can repeat. Processes are generally important in business, but when it's all down to you, they're imperative.

Depending on the project, the moving parts will vary, and we've provided some basic ideas here. No matter what, though, these are the elements where you'll need to focus your creative energy:

- Scheduling your calls
- Creating your project timeline
- Project content organization
- Ongoing client communication
- Writing
- Revising
- Maintaining version control

This list may seem overwhelming, but once you establish a process for your first project, it's just tweaks from there. For now, the next step is scheduling your next round of interview calls and developing a loose, general timeline for your project. If you share this timeline with your client, just make sure to tell them that it is subject to change.

TAKE ACTION

My Project Timeline Map

We've shared a bit about what works for us—now, it's time to define what works for you. How quickly do you want to work through a project? What kind of interview schedule suits you? Start mapping out your ideal plan, with the understanding that it will evolve over time as you gain experience.

Project Prep:	
Month 1:	**Month 2:**
Month 3:	**Month 4:**
Month 5:	**Month 6:**
Project Closeout:	

CHAPTER 15

The Art of Interviewing Clients

YOUR ROLE IN INTERVIEWS

The ghostwriter-client relationship is a tricky one, especially when you're starting out as a writer. But as you become more comfortable in your role, it can be incredibly fun and fulfilling. Although it may feel like you've developed friendships with these people after interviews, you absolutely cannot forget that they are paying clients. You're providing a service, and interviews are how you'll gather the information you need. Due to the nature of the service you're providing, the interviews will often delve into personal and professional topics that are close to their hearts. To ensure accuracy and thoroughness, it can be a good idea to record your calls (with their permission), so you can revisit conversations as needed. This helps you be more present in the meetings instead of madly trying to take notes. Alice writes this into all her contracts, so she doesn't have to ask for permission to record each call.

If you keep all this in mind during every single interview, even when it feels like you know their story better than your best friend's, you'll be okay. For example, both of us are jokers, but there is a time to joke and a time to hold a safe space. Remember that your client isn't family—they're not obligated to forgive you if you make a bad joke at the wrong time.

Ultimately, your job is to help tell their story, so every choice you make needs to keep that goal in mind.

The key is to remain the expert on the narrative throughout the entire process. As the interviewer, you can allow your client to process their emotions while guiding the conversation back to their purpose. You're responsible for processing the information, presenting it in a way that resonates with the reader, and anticipating the questions the reader might have. This skill is almost as important as the writing itself.

This is where your preparation is key. Even if you haven't received a lot of information from the client upfront, you need to have some questions ready for each interview. Not only will this help keep the conversation professional, but hopefully, it will encourage them to share their entire story with you.

You're never going to fully know someone's story until you dive in and ask about it. You can't expect to say, "So, tell me everything," and have them give you all the content you need for a book in chronological order, complete with details and emotion.

As the writer, you're the detective, gathering as much content as possible to capture their voice and create a compelling, linear narrative. This includes watching their body language, listening to verbal tones and cues, and paying attention to both what they share and what they don't. Instead of saying, "Tell me more about that," ask pointed questions about small details in the stories they share.

Keep in mind that if you joke or share any of your own personal story with the client, it should be intentional and purposeful. If you're building rapport and there's something relevant (and not overly intimate) from your own experiences that can aid in your mission, that's great. But don't get on a call with a client and rant about your shitty day or make a negative comment in the name of building trust. It's unprofessional and often regrettable. You are the guide in creating a space that is both professional and emotionally safe, and this balance begins the first time you connect.

Speaking of which, possibly the most important aspect of your role as the interviewer is active listening and asking thought-provoking, open-ended questions. Whether you're working on a memoir, business leadership book, self-help guide, or another genre, asking questions is only the beginning. Part of your job is to poke around, listen for clues, and follow where they lead—both in the moment and as you prepare for each subsequent interview. After that, adjust your approach accordingly.

MAKE SURE YOU GET THE STORY, EVEN IF YOU HAVE TO PULL IT OUT OF THEM

Every once in a while, even if you have the best questions in the world, you'll encounter a client who either A) isn't great at explaining or elaborating, B) has no idea what they actually want to say, or C) wants to tell you absolutely every detail about every part of their life, even when it isn't applicable to the project at hand. And these, my friends, are not fun challenges.

For Challenge A, you might have to call them out a little bit and be fairly direct. Try saying something like, "I want to tell your story, and for that, I need more complete answers to these open-ended questions. I can fill in the blanks, but I need content to start." These types don't love it, but they'll acquiesce.

Challenge B is a bit more complicated, because the client doesn't have a clear plan in mind. This problem often arises when someone wants to write a lead-generating book in self-help or business leadership but doesn't have much of a story to tell.

Undoubtedly, one of their peers or coaches has suggested they write a book as a marketing tool for their other ventures. So, you get to what you expected would be the meaty part of the interview and realize they don't have a method yet. Instead, they want you to reverse engineer their knowledge and success to extract a method where there wasn't one before. It's doable, but not ideal.

In many cases, you can let the client riff for 30 minutes and decode with something like, "What I'm hearing you say is this, this, and this." Most of the time, they'll respond with, "Yeah, that's it." Then, you can make it work.

Challenge C is when someone wants to tell you everything that has ever happened and finds it difficult to stay on topic. They may treat your sessions together more like therapy and less like a business relationship with boundaries. In these instances, you likely won't have a hard time getting details, but you will have to repeatedly steer the conversations back to the main story.

Alee: Madness with No Method

One of the most difficult projects I ever had was with a man who was extremely wealthy—debt-free, owned helicopters, the whole lot. He was a multi-multi-multi-millionaire, and he contracted with me to write a book about engineering your perfect life—going from a place of lack to a place of excess through vision boarding, manifesting, and similar concepts.

In the beginning, he told me he spoke on these topics all the time, but he never showed me anything concrete—just speeches about his wealth and success or podcasts where he discussed his lifestyle. He never actually explained what the method was.

After digging into his narrative through interviews, I realized he made his millions in a multi-level marketing scheme. In other words, he didn't have a method—he was selling a lifestyle he earned through a process that wasn't even his. No matter what I tried in the interview process, I just couldn't get anything meaningful from him. In the end, he said I was making him sound boring and blamed me for the lack of clarity in the book, then fired me.

HOLDING SPACE FOR BIG FEELINGS

First things first: Being someone's ghostwriter is not the same as being their therapist (even if you're career-switching from being a therapist). The reality is that when you're writing someone's story, it can get emotional. Striking the balance between responding compassionately and maintaining professionalism is another skill you'll need to develop. Early on, you might feel like you're in over your head—and you very well may be—but you'll also learn how to navigate it.

Alice: Learning How to Hold Space for Grief

There is one interview I will never forget. Earlier in my freelance career, I was writing a memoir for a woman who had experienced both spiritual and sexual trauma, and we met for an in-person interview. As she talked through her early experiences, she became completely overwhelmed by her grief. In the middle of the interview, she named her abuser out loud for the first time in her life. She slid out of her chair, melting down, sobbing, and rocking in a fetal position on the floor.

I literally had no idea what to do. Should I get her a tissue? Hug her? Sit with her? Since I wasn't sure, I decided to sit quietly, let her process, and wait it out. I sat in the room with her for what felt like ten minutes, allowing her to experience the emotions that were overwhelming her. It turns out it was the right move. After a few minutes, she calmed down, felt better, and was able to continue.

While I made the right choice, this experience pushed me to learn more about how to hold space for people dealing with grief and trauma while maintaining boundaries. It's a delicate thing— being charged with someone's most personal journey when you're not their mental health provider—and I never wanted to be caught off guard again, unsure of what to do.

If you end up writing on projects that involve traumatic experiences, it's a good idea to address the potential for strong emotions during your first interview. Before diving into the content, you can say something like, "I know you'll be discussing some difficult topics, and if you cry, get angry, or need to step away, this is a safe place to do that. After a few minutes, I'll usually prompt you with a completely random question to help pull you out of those emotions. I might ask you about the last time you spent time with your grandkids, or I might ask you about your dog. Please know that I'm not being insensitive—I'm simply trying to help you shift your focus from past emotions back to the present so that we can continue our conversation."

It sets the tone and reassures them that you've done this before, which helps them feel more comfortable—even though they often don't think they'll need the space until they do. Sometimes, when the moment is so powerful, you can't help but cry with them. That, too, shows them that this is a safe place to process emotions.

Alee: Using a Grief Questionnaire

Since I primarily work with stories of trauma and grief, I send out a specific questionnaire before I begin interviewing. One of the questions I include is, "What is the preferred response should you become emotional?" This helps eliminate any worry that I won't know how to handle it properly if the client starts to cry.

Also, in that document, I offer suggestions on how to prepare for a tough interview day and what to do afterward. For instance, a couple of scientific studies suggest playing Tetris as an activity to help ease trauma responses. The game is unique because it engages both the creative and pragmatic sides of the brain. Studies show that when trauma victims play it within a certain amount of time following a traumatic event, it can prevent

---

> *PTSD from setting in. This experiment was done in war zones with soldiers. Because of this, I suggest that my clients play an hour of Tetris or a similar game after our interview sessions. This gives them an opportunity to guard against potential post-traumatic stress if they feel triggered.*
>
> *I always say, "We are striving to create a safe, creative space, and it's not just for you, but for me as well." Some people react with anger when grief or trauma overwhelms them, so I preemptively tell clients that I don't do well with people who direct their anger toward me. This lets them know anger is not an acceptable reaction, and I will kindly and respectfully step away from the conversation and pick it up at another time.*

Journeying through conversations about trauma is always difficult, even when you have tons of practice. It's hard to watch another person relive their trauma as they tell their story. It's hard to watch someone cry. As the person facilitating the conversation, sometimes you just have to let them cry and be okay with the silence—both on your end and theirs.

We're often uncomfortable with silence, so we fill it with questions or statements of sympathy. But it's okay to just let it ride. Silence can be your best friend during tough conversations. Hold quiet space for their tears, and when it's time to proceed, press on gently. Just know that you may need to really work to get the details out.

Alee once had a client who was disfigured in a childhood accident. He was a very shy, soft-spoken, sweet guy—not a natural talker. He would answer questions in just one or two words. For example, when she asked him, "What was your mother like?" he would simply say, "Kind and generous." She had to probe further and ask more in-depth questions to get the fuller picture.

She learned from that experience to softly nudge people by asking direct and specific questions. For example, "Can you give me an example of a time when you experienced her kindness?" By doing this repeatedly, she trained him to answer her questions more fully. As they progressed deeper into the chapters, he became better prepared and more inclined to share information in greater detail. When she prompted him, he was quicker to recall things because she had guided him into a space where he could remember visceral details.

ADDITIONAL INTERVIEW CONSIDERATIONS

There are a few considerations you can include in your contracts when working with clients who will be sharing personally difficult stories. This isn't because you're anticipating a terrible experience, but because sharing these stories won't be a walk in the park.

First, you can address that this is not a replacement for therapeutic support or being under the care of a mental health provider. Additionally, some stories may turn out to be too difficult for a person to tell or may need to be withheld from the final manuscript for other reasons. It's also possible for your client to reveal information that puts you at legal risk—such as admitting to committing a crime—or ethical risk, particularly if you believe they are suicidal or pose a threat to themselves or others.

Having a "no fault" clause in your contract can be beneficial in these situations. This clause essentially states that if either party decides it's not the right fit, the relationship can be ended in writing with no hard feelings. It's rare, but it happens, and having this dynamic clause in place will be helpful if you (or they) ever need to exercise the option.

Another crucial point to address in the first meeting, especially when the story involves sexual abuse or self-harm, is to ask the client if they have a support team—such as a counselor or therapist—that they can speak to if they are triggered.

Alice once had a client whose whole life, in real-time, was going to absolute shit, and she felt there was no reason to keep going. Since Alice knew where she lived because of the contract, she looked up local resources, such as a suicide prevention hotline, and sent them to her via text and email. Alice has also had three clients who went to rehab during projects because they began abusing substances to numb the grief of their stories.

Life can be hard, even when someone's ready to write a book about it. Sometimes they'll come back to you after they've had time to process, and sometimes they'll never be ready to start again. Both are okay.

The key piece of advice here is to intervene if someone is at risk, but measure your intervention. You don't want to call the authorities unless there seems to be immediate danger. Often, providing resources and offering gentle support is the most reasonable approach.

Alee: Naming the Concerns

I've been in situations where I've said to clients, "I'm noticing some concerning responses when you become triggered. There's nothing wrong with those reactions, and there is no judgment from me, but it might be something for you to explore outside of our writing relationship—whether that be with a close friend or a professional."

The truth is, some of your prospective clients may say, "This is the next step in my healing journey," or, "This is like therapy." And they're right—it is like therapy, but it's important that they know it's not therapy and you are not their therapist.

TAKE ACTION

Tips for Ghostwriters Who Are Writing About Trauma

You don't know someone's story until you ask the right questions, and sometimes stories will be difficult for the client to share. Here are some tips to help you prepare for emotions and protect your own energy in the process:

1. Start by reassuring the client that it's okay to express their emotions and that you're happy to provide a safe space for them. Let them know you'll gently guide them back to the conversation when they're ready.

2. If you notice any signs of potential self-harm or other detrimental behaviors, bring them to their attention if you feel comfortable doing so.

3. If a client ever directs their anger or outbursts at you, that's a line crossed. You can remind them this is not a therapy session, and you do not appreciate being spoken to that way. You have the option to get off the call early, wait it out, and send an email later explaining that they can't speak to you in that way, or even cancel the contract if necessary (this is when a "no fault" clause comes in handy).

4. Make time for your self-care after difficult calls. Whether it's going for a walk, journaling, taking a break, or doing something that helps you get back to a positive headspace, prioritize your well-being.

CHAPTER 16

Writing the Manuscript

Isn't it funny that we're more than 100 pages in, and we're only just now talking about writing? That's the crazy thing about ghostwriting! There is so much work to be done in preparing, gathering information, and setting yourself up for success that the writing part ends up only being a portion of the process. Make no mistake, it's the **most important** part of the process, but in many cases, it feels like a relief to finally reach this stage, because you're finally getting to do what you love. Here, we'll break down every step so you'll build your first manuscript with ease.

TRANSCRIBING

Once your initial interviews are complete, you'll need to have the audio transcribed so you've got material to work from. While you can choose to work with a freelance transcriber, you may find that it is more expensive and time prohibitive than you'd like. Fortunately, there are plenty of websites that can transcribe your audio quickly for very little cost. Our favorite website to use is called Rev.com, but there are other options available. Additionally, Zoom now offers a feature that automatically outputs transcriptions of your calls.

DRAFTING

First and foremost, you need to decide how many words you're going to output at once. We prefer to start with a small deliverable (around 2,500 words) that can be used in discussions with clients. This smaller piece helps you agree on voice, tone, and pacing. After that, you can decide how much and how often you'd like to deliver the work. Alee likes to work in chunks of 5,000–10,000 words every two weeks, and Alice likes to write about 3,500–5,000 words each week.

First, open your outline and have it available. Copy and paste the relevant portion into a clean Word document. Then, open the transcriptions and copy and paste all relevant audio where it belongs according to the outline. Think of this as a very messy first draft.

Once that's in place, begin writing. Typically, we use the transcribed audio as a guideline for the story and chronology of events in order to write fresh content. Pay attention to the way the client naturally speaks and incorporate their language quirks. Stick as close to the story as you can, but allow yourself the freedom to fictionalize small details like the smell of the grass, the day's weather, and other elements that add color and texture to the piece.

INITIAL EDITING

Before you send your draft to the client, give yourself ample time to edit and revise. Typically, we recommend completing two rounds of substantive edits and one round of proofreading. We both write in Microsoft Word, which is standard for the publishing industry. We use the spellcheck feature first, and then we may also run the draft through a program like Grammarly. Those two programs usually catch the majority of mistakes. Then, we do another round of proofreading ourselves. If you're not a professional proofreader, which most of us are not, consider reading the manuscript backwards from the final chapter or final paragraph to the beginning. Reading out of order can often help you catch things you might've missed.

SUBMITTING TO THE CLIENT

Once you're satisfied with the draft, attach it to an email and send it to the client. (Alice likes to upload weekly chapters to Google Docs so the clients can edit the content while she's working on new chapters.) We like to include a reminder that this is the first draft of the content, there will be some typos and grammatical errors, and that we can expect to make lots of changes.

Encourage them to be extremely open with their feedback. At this point, it's crucial to ensure that the client is familiar with Microsoft Word and knows how to implement changes appropriately. This means making as many changes in-line as possible, using the Track Changes tool, and using the Comment feature for larger edits that they need your help with. If the client needs assistance navigating the program, consider giving them a crash course via Zoom or sending an instructional video.

FIELDING AND INCORPORATING THE FEEDBACK

Depending on who your client is and how they communicate, receiving feedback can be challenging. The key is to remember that there will be plenty of changes, no matter how seasoned you are as a writer. It doesn't mean that you're bad at your job; it means you're working hard to match your client's desired tone and get all of the tiny details right.

Start by reviewing the document with your client's changes and accept the easy ones (word choice, minor sentence tweaks, punctuation, etc.). Then, tackle the bigger comments. Familiarize yourself with them, then schedule a call to talk over any questions you have. One of Alice's clients has severe ADHD and prefers to talk through each chapter, allowing her to make edits to the Google Doc in real time during a video call. It's a unique approach, but it works.

Remember that clients will sometimes submit changes that are either grammatically incorrect, confusing, or don't add to the narrative in any meaningful way. As the expert, you have the right to mention any changes that don't serve the manuscript well. Just be open about this, and explain your reasoning. If the client disagrees, don't push it. Simply restate your case one more time, then remind them that it's their book, and they ultimately have the final say, regardless of your differing opinion.

REVISIONS

Finish incorporating all feedback and changes. This may require some rewriting, and that's okay. Keep reworking and refining until you feel confident it meets the client's expectations. Once that's done, perform another proofread, then send it back to the client.

MORE FEEDBACK

At this point, most clients will be happy to approve this chunk of words, but some may have an additional round of significant feedback. That's okay! Take a breath and repeat the same steps as above until the client is satisfied.

PUTTING IT ALL TOGETHER

You'll follow the process detailed above until you reach the desired word count. Once that's done, it's time to string everything together into a full manuscript. Start with a title page and a dummy copyright page (you can easily find a template online). They may begin with a title in mind, or they may not have one. You can keep a running list of titles and subtitles for them to choose from. Usually, by the end of the book, one title stands out above the rest.

Next, create a preliminary table of contents. It might sound surprising, but this is the ideal time for your client to start working on both the dedication and introduction. The introduction should come from them, speaking directly to the reader, welcoming them to the book, and sharing their hopes for the reader. You can either draft this for your client or ask them to write something from the heart that you can edit to perfection.

Again, there's no one way to do this. Alice always writes the introduction first, to set the tone of the book and ensure she's capturing the client's voice and goals. Then, once she's finished the manuscript, she'll revise it to ensure it says exactly what it needs to, based on the final manuscript.

READING IT THROUGH ONE LAST TIME

Once the introduction is complete and the manuscript is fully packaged, it's time for one last read-through. Have your client read the manuscript from beginning to end at the same time you do; you may even do this on a Zoom call or in person, if that's a possibility. We know several writers who conduct "table reads" with their clients, where they sit together and read it aloud. Once the read is complete, work together to reconcile your feedback and implement any last-minute changes.

EDITING (DEVELOPMENTAL, COPY EDIT, PROOFREAD)

Once this is complete, it's good practice to loop in an editor, and what that looks like is up to you. If this is your first book (or one of your first few books), you may choose to partner with a developmental editor to make bigger changes for clarity and flow. Most of the time, this isn't necessary, but if you have a client who has supplied so many edits that the book feels disjointed, bringing in someone who can help might be the right move. More often, the only thing you'll need is to have the book copyedited or proofread so the client walks away with something ready for publication!

HANDING IN YOUR WORK

Once the book is complete, it's time to hand in the final draft and say goodbye to your client. We typically send the final manuscript in both Microsoft Word and PDF formats. If you haven't yet, you can also include the final invoice in the same email.[3]

If you are helping them connect with a custom publisher or a self-publishing service, you can make that hand off now (or make those introductions while the book is being edited). If they want to pursue a traditional path, you can also help them write a query letter and a book proposal. (You can find query letter and book proposal templates online.) If you're interested in connecting them with literary agents, you can help them do that research as well.

Express how much you've enjoyed working with them, and mention that if they've enjoyed working with you and decide to refer others to you, they'll receive a referral fee. This is the perfect time to ask for an endorsement that you can use to find future clients.

Finally, let them know that you'll check in periodically to stay updated on how the book is performing in the marketplace.

---

[3] Important note: TRUST YOUR GUT! If you worry, even a little bit, that your client could skip out on the last invoice, ask to be paid in full before you release the final files. This is where that copyright clause in your contract comes in handy.

TAKE ACTION

Follow this checklist for completing your first draft:

☐ Transcribe your interviews.

☐ Copy and paste the relevant portion of the outline into a blank document.

☐ Open your transcriptions.

☐ Copy and paste relevant transcriptions into the outline.

☐ Begin writing using the transcriptions as your base.

☐ Edit.

☐ Proofread.

☐ Send to the client.

☐ Implement edits and feedback.

☐ Proofread.

☐ Send to the client.

☐ Implement edits and feedback.

☐ Repeat for all deliverables.

☐ Keep a list of possible titles and subtitles.

WRITING THE MANUSCRIPT

☐ Assemble the entire manuscript, including the title page, copyright page, table of contents, dedication, and introduction. Depending on the book, it may also have footnotes, endnotes, an appendix, or an index.

☐ Work with the client to choose a title and subtitle from the list.

☐ Do a final read-through.

☐ Do a final (professional) copyedit or proofread.

☐ Send the final draft to the client in Microsoft Word and PDF formats, and write an email as suggested.

☐ Make sure you receive the final payment before you hand over the final, edited files.

CHAPTER 17

AI: The Facts and the Future

We can't write a book about writing without addressing the elephant in the room: AI. In our opinion, it is here to stay. Yes, it's still a taboo/gray area for many in the industry. Some writers worry AI will soon take over all our jobs, and there will no longer be a need to hire professional ghostwriters. We have a different stance.

It is true that some people are using AI to write their books instead of hiring professionals, but it's also true that those books are pretty terrible, and you can absolutely tell that software was used in the creation. Why? It has no soul. It reads like a robot wrote it, with prose either too elevated and disconnected or too full of catchphrases that easily gives it away as artificially manufactured writing.

Alice will die on this hill (so check back with her in five years). She strongly believes that even if AI advances to the point that it can accurately represent a human personality and the complexities of storytelling, capturing tone and an author's quirks, there will still be plenty of people who, 1: are so distrustful of the technology that they prefer to hire a human ghostwriter anyway, and 2: really want the benefits of the ghostwriter-author relationship, because it creates a safe space similar to therapy with a built-in cheerleader and encourager.

One of the main reasons people hire a ghostwriter is that they don't want to have to sit at a desk and type out (or verbally rehash) their entire story as a lonely, solo act. They desire the collaboration and rich conversation, and they want to truly be seen by another person. AI can't replicate that.

While some publishers have a zero-tolerance policy regarding AI, others are taking the stance that AI should be used responsibly. We use AI in some form or fashion with every single project. For example, we use Rev.com for transcription—they offer a fast and cheap AI option that does a decent job. Even Microsoft Word and Grammarly are technically considered "corrective AI" products.

Some writers use AI to help them construct timelines or draft outlines of their story (when used to generate new content, this is called "generative AI"). And yes, some do use it to draft client chapters and entire books. Others use it to brainstorm ideas for opening scenes, for character development, and a myriad other pieces of the overall process.

Since it's still a murky area when it comes to legal copyright issues, you'll need to take a stance that feels comfortable to you and stick to it, while keeping up to date on the latest laws and regulations. And even though some publishers claim to use AI detection software, these products are not really that accurate.

Alice once wrote a personal story on her Substack and, for shits and giggles, uploaded it to an AI-detection site. It came back as "potentially 23% AI-written," which is a load of crap, because she's not a robot, even though she did absolutely have a childhood crush on Data from *Star Trek: The Next Generation*.

We believe that AI can be a brilliant tool to streamline your writing process and help you produce high-quality deliverables when used correctly. Alee uses it most often for two parts of the ghostwriting process: organizing content and providing critical feedback. Let's dive in to what they look like in practice.

ORGANIZING CONTENT (+ MAKING OUTLINES)

Organizing content is one of those things that can easily take hours when it doesn't need to. Of course, we know which story goes where—we were following along when the client explained it. But sometimes, when recounting complicated life events (especially traumatic ones) clients tend to hop around. They might be telling a story from the present, then relate it to a childhood event, then suddenly recall a conversation that needs to be placed earlier. When this happens, that conversation risks getting lost in the transcripts and not ending up where it needs to go in the book. Or, it makes its way into the outline, but the client has to repeat the story because we can't find the content. As an example, Alice once ghostwrote a self-help book with multiple authors based on 1,500 pages of transcript content. Yikes.

Wading through hundreds (or thousands) of pages of interview transcripts to find a three-paragraph conversation is the kind of task Alee might pass on to her editorial assistant or intern, but what happens when they're unavailable or she needs it immediately? She asks Claude (an AI that excels in nuanced text analysis) to do it for her. In a matter of seconds, she can have a clear, bullet point summary of the key events and direction as to where to look for the full discussion.

The same goes for quickly putting together outlines. The majority of this task is done during the interview process while the client is talking, but if she misses something or needs to make sure it's all correct, AI is a great tool to check her work.

PROVIDING CRITICAL FEEDBACK

AI can by no means replace the role of a thorough, experienced editor, but it can be a good way to improve your writing, especially in the early drafting stages. Have you ever felt like you've spent so much time with a chapter that you're blind to its faults? This is an excellent example of when it might be helpful to copy and paste it into an AI chat and ask for advice.

There are some tips and tricks to using AI assistants effectively, and it's all in the phrasing. We heard that a clever way to think of AI is like the genie from *Aladdin*. You have to be as precise and detailed as possible to get what you asked for—because it will misinterpret you at every chance it gets.

Here are some best practices for crafting prompts:

- **Be Specific**: Instead of "How can I make this better?" ask "How can I tighten this paragraph to reduce word count by 30% while maintaining the client's conversational tone and key message about leadership?"

- **Provide Context**: Always include relevant background information about your client, their target audience, and the project goals.

- **Use Examples**: When asking for style adjustments, provide examples of what you want to achieve or avoid.

- **Iterate**: Don't expect perfection on the first try. Refine your prompts based on the quality of the output. For example, if you ask for an outline and it's too long, or you want it in first person, ask the AI assistant to try again with that feedback.

- **Maintain Boundaries**: Remember that you're the ghostwriter with the client relationship—use AI for enhancement, not replacement of your expertise and judgement. To be clear, you should not have AI make improvements or changes for you. You are asking for guidance on the ways you can make the writing better.

Tailor every prompt to the text that you're working with and the specific blind spots you want the AI to pick up on. Then, take every suggestion with a pinch of salt. Even AI can get it wrong sometimes!

Remember, at the end of the day, you're the human here. You know what works in a way an AI doesn't (yet!). So, what's the bottom line? Keep your head down, do the work, write the content to the best of your abilities, and play around with AI tools as you see fit.

TAKE ACTION

AI is a powerful and valuable tool and creative partner that can enhance and assist with your work—but only if you know how to use it effectively. The key lies in crafting the right prompts that clearly convey exactly what you need.

Below are some example prompts you might consider using to get helpful feedback on your work. Try pasting a paragraph or chapter of your writing into your AI tool of choice, and then use a prompt such as:

- "Review this chapter for flow, logic, and engagement. Does the argument build effectively? Are there gaps in reasoning or missing examples that would strengthen the client's credibility?"

- "This section feels dry. Suggest ways to make it more engaging while keeping the professional tone my client needs for their [industry] audience."

- "Suggest edits to this passage for clarity, concision, and impact. I want to maintain the client's voice but tighten the prose and eliminate redundancy."

- "Check this chapter for consistency in terminology, tone, and the client's established viewpoints from earlier chapters."

Like any new tool, you'll need to experiment and practice to find the most effective ways to use it and how it can support (not replace) you the best.

CHAPTER 18

Building (& Billing For) Experience

When you first start ghostwriting, you may want to take on every project that comes your way. We've been telling you to do things like "niche down" and "define your audience," which is sound advice, and you should definitely do it once you're more established and have the flexibility (and the financial padding) to be choosier with your projects. On the flip side, we also understand that you need to survive, and you might not have the flexibility to implement these strategies right away. And that's perfectly okay.

Both of us jumped full-time into freelance writing from salaries that were livable but far less than what we wanted. Because neither of us was sure what our first year as freelancers would look like, we said yes to far too many different types of writing projects to ensure that we always had money coming in. This approach turned out to be extremely beneficial in more ways than one. Not only were we, thankfully, able to bring in enough money, but we were also able to discover what we loved doing and what we *never* wanted to do again. Some of it was invigorating, and some of it was draining.

You might find yourself taking a similar approach, and that's perfectly fine. However, it's important to always be discerning, even when you feel like you can't afford to be selective.

USE ALL EXPERIENCES TO YOUR BENEFIT (EVEN THE BAD ONES)

Maybe you'll get fired from a project. Maybe you'll quit one, or you'll finish a book but hate it every step of the way. It's important to know what you love and where you thrive; it's equally important to know what you hate, what you simply don't enjoy, and what drives you insane. There are lessons in every experience, and it's up to you to learn from them and act on those insights.

You owe it to yourself to create a list of all the things you loved or hated about a project, especially when you're gaining experience early on. Was it the client? Was it you? Was it the topic? Could you have fixed or changed something to make it better? Was the project a poor fit? What went wrong—and what went right? Do you need to add a clause to your contract to cover a new issue you experienced?

Give yourself permission to answer honestly, even if the answer is, "I guess I won't take that kind of project anymore." Every single ghostwriter in existence must go through this at some point. Even if you can write multiple genres, when you can finally afford to write what you love, do more of that. And if you're still in a traditional job waiting to break free, start making a list of the tasks and topics you excel at and love, and which ones you can't stand.

> ### *Alee: Getting Fired Helped Me Find My Niche*
>
> *Early in my career, I took on a bunch of very dry, clinical books, and each project ended the same way: fired, fired, fired. I sort of knew it wasn't my thing, but clearly so did my clients. Even though it made for a bit of a bumpy ride, accepting everything right out of the gate helped me quickly discern what I did and did not want to do in the long-term. I came to understand that I'm not suited for books that educate without much personality or storytelling. Recognizing that fact has helped me curate a project list that I love!*

LEVERAGING "UNRELATED" EXPERIENCES

No matter what your life has been like before venturing into the realm of ghostwriting, your experiences matter. Often, writers downplay or even hide their non-writing experiences. But if you get creative, you can leverage many of those experiences as relevant to your writing career—and many clients will appreciate you even more for them.

Alee: Leading a Grief Group

I am extremely open about living with bipolar disorder and CPTSD. These conditions have profoundly shaped my life, but with consistent medication, therapy, and psychiatric care, I manage them effectively. When working with prospective clients who are navigating mental health challenges or trauma recovery, I share this part of my story. While these topics remain taboo in most professional settings, my transparency creates an immediate bridge of understanding. Clients feel deeply seen because they recognize that I truly understand their struggles—not just intellectually, but experientially. I've walked through similar symptoms, side effects, and dark moments. This shared understanding of the landscape allows me to write their stories with an authenticity and depth that comes from lived experience.

This doesn't stop at relevant personal experience. You can leverage your non-book-writing jobs, even if they seem totally irrelevant. Alee, for instance, spent time in the fashion industry—a high-pressure, tough environment, to say the least. It's not writing, but when she needs to demonstrate her grit to a client, she mentions it.

She also spent time writing catalog copy for jewelry and fashion brands. While it might seem irrelevant to book writing, there are nuggets that apply. Writing copy for clothing requires astute attention to details you might not have noticed otherwise. The copy always followed a formula, like "Throw on this wool jacket and head out for..." But to make it compelling, she had to envision the life of someone wearing that tweed jacket and craft a vivid, engaging story in as few words as possible. It's not a memoir, but it's storytelling, nonetheless.

Leveraging your experience means taking the time to review your entire education and career for every teeny, tiny nugget related to writing, connecting with people, holding challenging conversations, and creating structure where there was none. From there, you mold each nugget into something pertinent to your business.

It's important to take this part seriously. You never know whether the things you consider insignificant might actually give you an edge over everyone else.

WHAT IS WORTH DOING FOR FREE OR CHEAP?

At the beginning of your writing career, it may be tempting to give away your services for free or at a significant discount to build your portfolio and gain experience. This is fine to an extent, especially if it's *your* idea to offer the discounted or free work. However, be intentional with these choices and recognize when you're being taken advantage of.

Some people will flat-out ask you to work for free, claiming it'll be great for your exposure and your portfolio. It's a trap! Don't fall for it! Unless you genuinely want to work on their project, and have written permission to include it in your resume and portfolio—so you can at least gain some benefit from the free work—just say no.

When Alice first started out, she did a lot of writing pro bono (which is just a fancier way of saying "for free") and took on other projects for very little money. This was partially because the jobs she accepted had small budgets, and because she had no idea what others in the industry were charging. She rarely agrees to pro bono work now, but on the very rare occasion when an agent or a client asks for a one-page sample, she considers it if she *really* wants the project.

While you're not obligated to do anything for free, you can also take the bull by the horns and turn these situations into networking opportunities. For example, you could approach people in your field who you admire and offer to write a couple of blog posts or a small ebook for them at either no charge or minimal pay, with the understanding that you'll be able to include the work in your portfolio.

If you offer to do something like that, it's a lower time investment than an entire manuscript, obviously, but it provides the same reward in terms of gaining experience and adding a portfolio piece. You might also ask for an endorsement for your website in return, or say, "If you ever come across someone who needs a ghostwriter, please pass them my way. I'm happy to pay a referral fee!"[4]

Essentially, if you're going to do something for super cheap (or nothing at all), make sure it's worth your while. Be intentional and take control. Remember, you're always working to grow your business—this isn't just a hobby, even if your goal is to write part-time.

WHEN TO STOP DOING THINGS FOR FREE OR CHEAP

First things first, especially once you're established: If the same person repeatedly asks you to work for free or for "exposure," run. Discernment rears its head again. Early on, these opportunities might seem beneficial, but there's a thin line between being lifted up and taken advantage of. Anytime you agree to steep discounts, be clear from the start about what the end product will be, the project's parameters, and whether this is a one-time deal—and get all of that in writing. Verbal agreements hold zero weight in publishing or any other industry.

Sadly, there's no magic number of projects or set timeline for when you should stop considering free or lower-paying work (if you even consider it to begin with), or when and how often to raise your prices.

---

[4] We talk more about referral fees in Chapter 11.

But once you've built a strong portfolio, it's time to remember that you're a professional writer with a professional business, and your purpose is to make money.

You may say to yourself, "I will never, ever do anything for free or for far less money." But sometimes, projects come along that are worth bending that rule for. Don't let those opportunities pass you by, but these will likely be rare. When writing becomes your livelihood, you should be working for money rather than exposure or experience.

As you advance in your career, people may still ask for free or discounted services, but you get to be much more selective about whether you say yes. Even after twenty-five years in the industry, Alice is occasionally asked for a free sample of work because the client wants to see what she's capable of before signing a contract. She very rarely agrees to this. Instead, she sends several writing samples from previously published books, allowing the client to see how she has brought other stories to life on the page.

This is always a judgement call, depending on what you need, what you want, and how much time you're able to invest in requests for free or lower-priced work. These factors will vary in importance throughout your career. Remember, your time is your greatest commodity, so working for free or for little money is not something you *have to do*.

If there's a passion project you believe in and you want to be flexible with your rates, there's no right or wrong answer. It's your business. Ultimately, what's "worth doing for free or cheap" is a judgement call that will likely fluctuate depending on where you are financially, personally, and professionally.

Alice: Agreeing to Less Money for a Great Story

As with most general statements, there are exceptions. Several years ago, I finished a book with an author for a significantly smaller fee than I typically charge. Her story focused on a cause

---

> *I feel strongly about, and since she couldn't afford my regular rate, we reached a different agreement. The result was less income for me, but the project was easy and fulfilling, and I was honored to help her share her story. That's a win-win for both of us.*

WORKING WITH FRIENDS AND FAMILY

Starting out, close personal relationships can be tricky to navigate, because your friends and family have likely known you longer as a person than as a writer. They see you as someone starting a new career, so they may not fully understand or value the rates you set—or even realize those rates exist.

So, if Great Aunt Erma wants to recount her memories of being a mechanic in World War II, by all means, please record all her stories and help her put together a legacy project for the sake of history *if you want to*. However, if your best friend's cousin asks you to write free blogs about her accounting business and *you don't want to*, that may be a great time to politely decline.

Sometimes projects with friends and family can be beneficial. If you want to focus on memoir, adding a legacy memoir to your portfolio could be valuable. If you're interested in ghostwriting blog posts, an accounting blog might be a great place to start. It all depends on your niche.

Ask yourself: If I say yes to this project, will it be mutually beneficial? Is it relevant to my goals? Will it strengthen our relationship or drain me? Could it lead to resentment? Discernment and boundaries are key.

> ### *Alice: Referring Out Family and Friends*
>
> *Years ago, a friend asked me to work on a project, and because she was a friend, I automatically discounted my rates in my head before I even told her what they were. This led to resentment*

on my part from the start, through no fault of hers. Setting these boundaries used to be tough for me—a blind spot, if you will—and I prefer not to accept projects from family and friends anymore. It can be awkward to say no and refer them to another writer, but it saves the relationship from potential drama in the long run.

TAKE ACTION

Spin Your Experience

Whether you're fresh out of school or transitioning from a completely different career, you have valuable experience to leverage. It's time to pull out the stops, take a hard look at your resume, and become your own spin team!

Use the questions below to help you think out of the box:

- What has your work experience made you an expert in, and why?

- What classes have you taken, whether in school or otherwise, that challenged you and broadened your knowledge? How?

- What groups are you a part of that might help you write the content you're most interested in?

- What special interests and hobbies do you have?

- What is something you know that others might not?

- What topics have you informally educated yourself about (or would like to) (e.g., with TED Talks, MasterClass, other online resources)?

Remember that this isn't about pretending to be someone you're not, it's about digging deep and recognizing the breadth of experience you can bring to the table to best tell your client's story.

CHAPTER 19

Evaluating and Overcoming
Your Blind Spots

You're not going to be good at writing every kind of book.

There, I said it.

When you first start freelancing, it can be tempting to treat every project as equally important. Someone might ask you to write a book about making socks, another about their relationship with their mom, and a third about financial planning. Since these are all viable, paying projects, you'll want to do it all, and you'll want to give each one your full attention. But the reality is, you'll be better at some things than others.

Of course, you should stretch yourself and try different types of projects, especially when you're first starting out. However, as you explore, it's important to quickly learn how to prioritize and choose your projects based on your interests and skills.

LEARN TO DISCERN

If technical business books are your thing, more power to you. Alee struggles with anything dry or academic, while Alice excels at narrative, mission-based business books but steers clear of sales funnel technology-related business theory, or political topics. We know our blind spots and where our skills don't shine, and we avoid pursuing projects we don't believe we're best suited for.

It's also important to recognize how your life experiences will impact the projects you choose to keep or pass along. As a ghostwriter, you're often writing about experiences you haven't personally had. While you don't need to limit yourself to clients who look like you or share your background, it's crucial to consider whether your core life experiences— or lack thereof—might affect your ability to tell their stories in an authentic, natural way.

An essential part of developing awareness around blind spots is admitting when your personal perspective or experience might weaken your writing, especially if someone else could do the content more justice.

For example, Alee was once asked to do a book with a public figure whose views she couldn't get behind. Though the project promised fantastic money and great exposure, she knew her personal views would make it nearly impossible to do his content justice, so she declined.

Likewise, Alice was once asked to write a book about natural hair care for women of color. She could have researched the topic extensively, but instead, she chose to refer the author to another writer who had the cultural knowledge and life experience and was a perfect fit for the project.

OVERCOMING YOUR BLIND SPOTS

When making decisions about potential projects, it's crucial to have the full picture—and that means honestly assessing your limitations and blind spots as well as your client's. Personal and professional growth, along with achieving your full potential as a writer, depends on this self-awareness. Adjusting your approach when necessary is one of the best (and hardest) ways to elevate your business.

Step 1: Surround yourself with a diverse group of people and ask for feedback.

Some people align themselves only with others who share the same views, but we encourage you to go against the "birds of a feather" thing. In this business, it benefits you to be around other writers and editors who think differently from you so you can get an authentic and helpful critique of your blind spots.

Step 2: Keep your ego in check as you assess the feedback.

Don't make any moves right away. Take some time to consider the information that you've received. Then, trust and value the perceptions of those friends and colleagues you've purposefully placed in your circle.

If someone gives you criticism, a great way to respond is, "Thank you for letting me know." At that point, take a step back and be introspective. This is not the time to lash out or be angry, even if it stings a little (more on this in a bit). It's imperative that you use their feedback, even when it's unexpected and uncensored, to refocus and adjust your trajectory, even if that ultimately means ignoring their feedback altogether. The only way you'll conquer your blind spots is to be intentional and reflective.

Step 3: Make a plan to improve and put it into action.

The last step is to chart a path forward. Take accountability for the things you can control, such as paying more attention to editing or adding details, and begin to foster goals that support the change you're making.

Be sure that this plan outlines specific actions you're going to take to improve the area where growth is needed. Make sure those actions are achievable and measurable. The best way to see success is to start off with a very simple action plan so you can really see the results. Success garners confidence, which in turn, garners more success.

RESPONDING VS. REACTING

Criticism holds a special sort of sting when you're a creator, so taking a solution-oriented, proactive approach gives you a bit of control you'll desperately feel you need in these situations. Don't make excuses; take ownership of what you should take ownership of, and open the discussion. You're not going to get the writing perfect every time, and it hurts. But the sooner you accept that, the sooner you'll be able to handle criticism like a pro.

Responding thoughtfully is key. Before you do, pause and think about what you'll say before it slips out of your mouth. Take a walk around the block with your dog. Scream into a pillow. Do a quick meditation exercise. Do whatever you need to do to get grounded. When you feel calmer and less reactive, you can ask the right questions to understand the problem without letting your emotions take over. If you react immediately, all that goes out the window, and your client may go out with it.

When you try your hardest, at the very least, you come to the table knowing you're not failing due to a lack of effort. It doesn't mean you're not talented or that you're bad at your job. It doesn't even mean you've failed. It just means the tactic you're using isn't working for the situation. It's important to keep a little distance from that self-berating voice and replace it with, "You've got this!"

So, if a client expresses that something you've written feels off, that you haven't properly captured their voice, or one of the other million possible issues they may have, start your response by asking questions like:

- Are there any specifics you can offer about what seems disconnected?

- What could I have done differently?

- How can we make this more successful moving forward?

Then, make a plan to do something about it. Let them know you hear them. Take another shot. Try again, even if your ego is bruised.

REPLACE "SORRY" WITH "THANK YOU"

Replace the word "sorry" with "thank you." When someone is unhappy, instead of apologizing effusively (writing is subjective as it is, so what are we sorry for?), say, "Thank you so much for communicating this. I hear you. Let's work together to get this right. There's nothing that we can't fix, so let's just backtrack." Then, you can focus on collaboration.

Saying you're sorry may seem nice, but it doesn't accomplish anything productive. Sometimes, clients complain that you got the details wrong and assign all kinds of meaning to this about your ability. Listen, sometimes we get things wrong! It happens. Sometimes, details are wrong because you misunderstood either their words or their intent. Sometimes it's because they gave you the wrong information.

When you say sorry, you're accepting blame, not taking ownership. When you say *thank you* and then go back into your transcripts, it's more neutral and less defensive, if you eventually have to tell them you were, in fact, given incorrect information.

Alee: On Accepting Criticism

I once had a client working on a grief recovery guide. Her methodology was crystal clear in her mind, but her communication was murky. During our initial interview, I felt confident we were a good match—she seemed really nice, and I believed I could help her translate her vision into compelling prose.

As we dove deeper into the project, I found myself struggling to extract what she really wanted to say. No matter what I did or how many clarifying questions I asked, I just wasn't nailing

---

it. Soon, she grew increasingly comfortable pointing this out. No matter how many manuscript versions I delivered—complete with major revisions, extensive edits, and thousands of new words—she'd respond with comments like, "When are we going to start doing the work?"

I was baffled. From my perspective, I was submitting substantial work with each deliverable. But no matter how hard I tried, I couldn't seem to get the project on track to her satisfaction. She eventually became furious with me for not "producing," though I could never pinpoint exactly what was missing.

We'd locked ourselves into a hopeless cycle: I couldn't intuit what she wanted, and she couldn't articulate her actual vision clearly enough for me to capture it. I was giving everything I had, but I simply wasn't the right ghostwriter for her project. So, I owned it. We worked together to find an equitable way to end our professional relationship, and I learned a valuable lesson about recognizing when a project isn't the right fit.

RECOGNIZE WHEN YOU'RE TRIGGERED

Writers who choose to be writers are not doing this because it's easy money. We do it because we love the craft and believe we have skills to offer. It's personal, even though it's professional, and there's no way around that. So, no matter how much we understand that criticism is inevitable, it's entirely possible we'll be triggered when negative feedback strikes.

You may find yourself in a personal battle with your confidence because you were hurt, despite your action-based approach. You may be scared to send back your second draft because you're now second-guessing your very existence in this field.

People may criticize you for things they don't recognize are their fault. It's hard to tell our own stories with complete accuracy, and sometimes clients don't realize this until they read your work—and they might blame it on you.

Have a plan for when this happens. Criticism can mess with you.

CLIENT COMPLAINTS AND CASH

We'll touch on this when we discuss The Perfectionist in a bit (Chapter 19)—but some clients may be so displeased that they want discounts, refunds, etc. It's the worst. We've said this more than once: This is a subjective business. The reality is, you could produce pure gold, and someone could hate it with a passion. Or, they could really like it but simply not want to pay you, so they lie and say your writing is trash. Not everyone is going to like your writing, but the key in this business is finding out as early as possible if you're in a situation that you cannot remedy.

Just remember, "I don't like it" is not specific feedback unless it's followed by a reason. And even then, give it another go. As mentioned earlier, you should start the writing process by sending the client's first chapter for approval. If they're not happy after three or more attempts, it's time for them to find another writer.

No one needs to waste their time if it's a terrible fit. We don't like to refund them for any work we've already done unless there are extenuating circumstances, but we also won't triple the work with a client we'll never be able to satisfy.

> ### *Alice: Regretting Refunds*
>
> *Full disclosure, because one size never fits all—I've given refunds I shouldn't have. Many years ago, I did an editing job for a client with health issues, which she was writing about. She*

was happy with my work throughout the process. When I sent her the final manuscript, she paid the final invoice, and I didn't hear anything back from her.

Three years later, she sent me a scathing email. She said she'd finally gotten around to reading the manuscript and found an excess of typos.

"I can't believe you charged me for this!" she wrote. "You took advantage of my health situation. I demand a refund."

I had never received an email like this before. I looked through the manuscript again in depth (and used spell check and Grammarly) and didn't see any errors. So, I asked if she could point them out for me, but she said she didn't have time. I even offered to pay for an additional copyedit out of my pocket.

She refused.

I started to suspect she just might really need money due to her situation, and I was scared she'd say something mean about me online.

So, three years after the fact, I gave her a large portion of her money back, even though I had zero proof that anything was wrong with the manuscript. In the end, I could afford to give her a portion of the money back, so I did.

It's worth noting that if a similar situation happened now, I would approach it much differently.

POST-CRITICISM CARE

When hurtful criticism happens, have a post-incident care plan. Journaling can help you reflect. Write out what happened and the criticism they offered, then review the communication and see if you can pinpoint where things went wrong. Sometimes you can, and sometimes you can't. But it helps. So do tacos. And fries.

You can also write your knee-jerk, unfiltered reaction in a blank document and leave it for a day. We probably don't need to say this, but we will anyway: Do *not* send this document to anyone. The next day, read your response, and see what the feedback triggered. Then, take action.

You may never be great at accepting criticism; you just learn how to better manage your emotions and reactions when it happens. Maybe you bounce back faster, or maybe you only eat *half* a tub of Ben & Jerry's as you question every decision you've ever made. (If you do this, Alice suggests Chocolate Chip Cookie Dough.)

Even though you give your best effort every time, not all projects will be winners and not all your clients will love you. And that's okay.

It's important to say that outright. You're human—we all are. And it doesn't matter how long you're in the business. You will still make mistakes. You will be fired. You will let clients go. That's life. That's business. Keep going anyway.

Alice: When Feedback Makes You Doubt Your Ability

I had a client years ago whose story was difficult to streamline. The client berated me, telling me I wasn't taking his book seriously, and I felt completely deflated halfway through the project. Despite the praise I'd received from my previous ten clients for how well I'd captured their voices, I couldn't separate myself from this guy's hurtful words. They hit me right in the maybe-I-am-a-crap-writer bone.

So, I reached out to Alee. I reached out to other close colleagues. I ate my weight in Mexican food. I wallowed for a full day. I thought about it. I worried about it. Somehow, by the next morning, I realized that his criticism said more about him and his ego than it did about me and my ability to write well.

TAKE ACTION

List of Compliments

One thing that helps us immensely is keeping a list of compliments we've received to refer to when someone says something unkind. This list is made up of golden nuggets that lift our spirits and remind us why we chose this career. Take some time to list the compliments you've received about your writing in the space below.

What nice things have been said about you and your writing? If no one has said anything wonderful about your writing yet, what are some of the most recent compliments you've received in general?

1.

2.

3.

Post-Project Checklist

While it's truly hard to know what you don't know, reflecting on your blind spots is an important part of this business. Look back at your previous body of work and note the times you felt exhilarated versus times you felt drained.

Project Title	Feelings about the Project	Project Content/ Description	Feelings about the Client Relationship

CHAPTER 20

Sticky Situations and Red Flags

Most of your clients will be incredible, level-headed, perfectly wonderful people. A select few will be problematic. It's really a numbers game until you're great at listening to your intuition and setting boundaries. The longer you do this work, the lower your chances are that you'll encounter a less-than-ideal situation (although it still happens now and then).

Unfortunately, helping a client journey through grief compassionately isn't the only intense or potentially uncomfortable situation you'll encounter as a ghostwriter. The cringe potential is real across all manner of stories encompassing the human experience. And, as with all relationships and interactions, things can get really weird, really fast.

While you might not always be picky when first starting out, you should still be on the lookout for red flags—and, if you notice them, trust your gut. When we look back at some of our own sticky client situations, there were almost always alarm bells going off early on that we ignored for one reason or another. If your internal alarm is telling you the client is a creep you don't want to write for, they're probably a creep you don't want to write for.

While it's not a perfect directory, there are some tried-and-true red flags you'll encounter throughout your ghostwriting career—and while it's ultimately your decision whether to say yes or no, don't let yourself get blindsided.

Alee: The Creep

I once had a client I ended up firing for a myriad of reasons, but the final nail in the coffin was his real-time sexual experience during one of our interviews. As he described an intimate moment he wanted to write about, he actually started to moan. And I mean "moan" in the way you think I mean moan. I literally mouthed "Oh my God" in horror as I listened over the phone on our recorded call. Ick.

I COMPLETELY froze in the moment, but immediately afterward, I emailed the project manager of the agency and said, "FYI, this just happened, and I am not comfortable with it." I fired the client that day.

THE CRIMINAL

This is one of the more serious red flag client types. You may run across potential clients who lead you to believe they are the reason for government anarchy or that they have information on someone in the political or entertainment industry. Be careful. Weigh your options before you agree to move forward. Is the money worth the risk of becoming a potential target if the book upsets someone violent or litigious? You may ultimately answer yes, but don't make that decision until you've really thought through the potential fallout (also consult your lawyer).

This also goes for people who want to write about their borderline questionable or flat-out illegal activities. People will tell you some crazy things, and depending on what it is, you may or may not be comfortable with that level of risk. Red. Flag.

Alice: The Murder Memoir

I once had a conversation with a man who wanted to write a tell-all that included several mafia-related murders. He'd done some jail time and supposedly worked out a plea bargain, but he essentially wanted help authoring a detailed confessional. I couldn't do it (and my lawyer agreed I shouldn't), but another writer may have thought the risk was worth the reward and jumped at the chance.

Alee: Dealing with a Jerk

I once had a client who was perfectly nice, but I soon came to realize that her story had elements that made my skin crawl. Her narrative included a long period of tension between her and her husband, and the conflict was pivotal to the story, but I found it hard to understand what actually caused it. After several interviews, she asked me to schedule some time where she and her husband could sit down with me together and explain what happened. It turned out that the conflict was kicked off by a sexual assault the husband committed, although he was never convicted. They wanted me to include the struggles they went through, but they wanted me to help fictionalize a reason for the tension to avoid anyone suspecting the husband of a crime. I left the meeting feeling sick. It makes me feel gross to admit this, but I stuck with the project and helped them craft a lie. And wouldn't you know it, after expressing gratitude, the client tried to wiggle out of her last payment. This project changed me—I vowed never to suppress my morals again.

THE PERFECTIONIST (WHO WILL FIND ANY REASON TO GET OUT OF PAYING IN FULL)

There are clients who expect perfection—from word choice to page numbers. They want everything exactly right, typically the very first time. Often, they're the ones who ultimately define what "right" is, which isn't inherently wrong. The problem is that they often have zero grace or patience to see the project for what it is—a process. These people cannot be satisfied. Writing is subjective, and you're not an editor. If someone doesn't understand either of these principles, you should reevaluate.

If you get a sense early on this may be the case with a client, you might not automatically walk away, but you should consider if they're going to make your life a hell of a lot harder. Part of the screening process for this particular red flag is to tell clients from the start that you strive to create a safe, creative space for *both them and you*. This includes kind, calm, and respectful communication when they have concerns as well as an understanding that you're not a copyeditor or a proofreader.

This approach has been helpful in managing clients who freak out with complaints like, "You sent this to me, and there are no page numbers!" Or who panic because you didn't get their voice exactly perfect in every single sentence the first time.

If you catch wind they've already worked with other writers and terminated previous relationships because they didn't like the work, ask more questions. Yes, bad writers exist, but more often, this is less about the writer and more about the client. Often, clients like these only have complaints with no specific suggestions for changes other than, "It's just not right. Do something else." You will never win. Without actionable feedback, these clients create stalemates that often allow them to walk away with far more of your work than they've paid for.

THE PATIENT

While Alee encounters this more frequently due to the nature of the books she writes, many people who want to tell their story are in recovery from addiction or have mental health issues. Your heart may go out to them, but it's important to maintain at least some layer of practicality. In the end, this is a business deal.

For instance, if someone is a recovering addict, ask them where they are in their sobriety journey and how confident they feel about it. Pay attention if you sense they aren't actually sober—and definitely pass on the project if that is the case. Of course, there's always a chance of slippage, but getting a sense of their self-perception is important, especially because they'll be journeying through their traumatic past. It's important to know if they have a support system (such as a therapist or a psychiatrist).

THERE CAN ONLY BE ONE—AND IT'S ME!

You may have clients who say something like, "I want to wait to work with you until I'm the only client you have." They might volunteer to wait until you're done with every other project you're working on. They insist that they need your undivided attention. In other words, they want to own and control you while you work on their project. (Revisit Chapter 12 for a refresher on these one-and-only clients.)

Now, some writers do work on only one project at a time, and that's great. For those writers, these clients aren't a problem. However, most writers work on more than one project at a time for financial reasons.

If someone wants this level of control over your time, it's important to keep the boundaries clear and simple. You don't need to tell them exactly how many projects you're working on, but you do want to reassure them that you'll give the project the time and attention it deserves.

However, you have to remember that the attention it deserves is not 24/7. You're allowed to have other projects, and you're allowed to have a life with normal business communication hours and methods. That's why you became a freelancer in the first place. All of that said, if a client really does want to be your only focus, and you really want the project, come up with a fee that matches their expectation—this might mean you charge them the rate you'd typically charge for two or three books.

THE CRUSH OR WANNABE BFF

No matter the chemistry, real or manufactured, some clients will attempt to flirt with you or try to be your new bestie. (Spoiler alert: It's usually because they want a discount.)

You'll have to decide what you're comfortable with on a case-by-case basis. Clients may invite you out to dinner. Great! Who doesn't love food?

They may also offer to pay for dinner. That's also great. (If you pay, make sure you write it off.)

Dinner at their house? Depends on whether you feel comfortable.

Dinner at your house? Again, your call. We rarely ever invite clients to our homes (unless they're dropping off a signed copy of the book we finished together), and we do not conduct any in-person meetings in our home offices.

Clients may offer for you to stay with them if you travel to meet them for in-person interviews. Instead, ask them to cover the cost of your hotel. Also, think twice before drinking or hanging out with a client until after the book is done.

Unfortunately, some clients will try to lean heavily on the "we're such good friends!" bond that can develop during the process, using you for therapy sessions and discussing things that have nothing to do with the book. Again, that's where those boundaries really help.

However, it's entirely possible you might become actual friends with a client post-book. Both of us have clients-turned-buddies-turned-extended-family. You get to decide what feels right to you.

THE ABUSER

The biggest disaster client Alee had fell into the abuser category, and she ignored red flags all over the place.

Alee: The Erratic, Angry Client

When the client first emailed me, I told her my schedule was so full that there was no way I could take her project on. Her book was essentially an exposé of crimes she committed and got away with, which wasn't a great start as far as her character was concerned. But I chose to view it as the story of a person who has never felt heard, and I took it on anyway.

She had so much written that I thought it would mostly be about piecing things together and editing. In my mind, it would be pretty straightforward. Oh man, was I wrong. Things started smoothly enough, but they began to unravel quickly. The first deliverable was a breeze, but soon she became highly erratic. I would submit work to her on Monday, and we'd have meetings on Tuesday where she would rave about how amazing the deliverable was. By Thursday, she would hate everything, get angry, and start berating me.

I just wanted to finish the book. We'd contracted for a total of 30 phone hours and 70,000 words and, of course, I priced the project accordingly. It should have been cut and dry. It was not. In the end, I spent more than 100 hours on the phone with her and submitted a manuscript of 96,000 words, which I fully packaged

---

with a cover because I knew she liked tangible things. After she received it, I was expecting a somewhat positive response. Instead, what I received was the following email: "None of the edits we discussed are in here. This is complete trash."

I had done everything I could, and making it better was clearly not an option. So, I gracefully stepped away. And while I'm proud of myself for standing up to her, I also know that if I'd paid attention to the signs early on, I never would have worked with her in the first place. It would have saved me hours of despair, self-doubt, and an unbelievable amount of stress.

Alice: The Client Who Sent Me to Therapy

Early in my ghostwriting career, I signed a project with a woman who wanted to become a life coach and her book was about a coaching system she developed that was based on addressing generational trauma. Sounded intriguing enough.

I hadn't yet learned how to set boundaries or how many hours of interviews and in-person meetings were needed for a whole manuscript. She started dictating how frequently we met (3 times a week and for 4-hour blocks at a time). I didn't feel like I could say no.

Next, she started frequently disrespecting me, commenting on my "boring" conservative clothes, my weight, my hair, and all the reasons why a man wouldn't want to date me. All of this, of course, was said under the guise of coaching me on her system.

After several months of torture and with my self-esteem non-existent, I had to quit the project, get my lawyer involved, and start going to therapy to deal with how terrible I felt about myself.

PROACTIVELY SET YOUR BOUNDARIES

We've talked a lot about the level of familiarity that can develop when working so closely with someone and hearing their story one-on-one. In this profession, it's crucial to understand your own boundaries and ensure that those you're collaborating with do as well. As you consider boundaries, ask yourself the following questions:

1. What modes of communication am I comfortable using with clients? (This includes phone calls, video calls, texting apps, and emails.)

2. Will I have set days and hours during which I will respond to communications?

3. Will I be available in the evenings or on weekends for meetings?

4. How quickly will I respond to clients? (Alee has a communication policy of 24 hours on weekdays and 48 hours on the weekends Alice still sometimes struggles with the desire to send instantaneous responses, but has gotten better over the years.)

5. Will there be topics I deem off-limits in projects I accept or in client discussions?

6. How will I communicate my boundaries with clients, and how will I address any issues clients have with respecting my boundaries?

WHEN IT'S TIME TO WALK AWAY

At some point in your ghostwriting career, you'll inevitably encounter a situation where you need to part ways with a client. While it's never fun, knowing how to handle these moments professionally can save your sanity and your reputation.

If you've reached an impasse where continuing the project would be detrimental to both you and your client, it's time to cut ties. The key is doing so with grace and professionalism, even when you're frustrated or hurt.

HAVING THE CONVERSATION

If you have a decent working relationship with the client, consider having this conversation via phone or video call. Keep it straightforward and professional. We've found the phrase "Unfortunately, we have reached a stopping point" to be particularly effective—it's clear without being accusatory.

However, if you don't trust yourself to stay calm during a live conversation, or if the client has been volatile, stick to email. Write a firm but kind message that outlines your decision without getting into the messy details of why.

Your contract should outline termination terms, but in practice, you'll likely need to get creative to find a solution that works for everyone. If you're the one ending the relationship, consider being more generous than you might normally be to avoid major conflict. This might mean refunding a portion of your fee or handing over more work than the contract requires.

Remember, you can't control how they're going to react. Some clients will be understanding, while others might unleash their fury via email or threaten to trash you online. Prepare yourself mentally for various scenarios, including an angry blowup, even if it seems unlikely.

If you're working through an agency, don't go rogue. Involve them in this decision from the start and let the agent lead the termination process. They have experience navigating these situations and can often smooth things over better than you can on your own.

The bottom line? Sometimes walking away is the best gift you can give both yourself and your client. Trust your instincts, handle it professionally, and move on to projects that are a better fit.

GREEN FLAGS: SUCCESS STORIES AND WHY WE DO WHAT WE DO

Remember, most of your clients will be absolute gems, and you'll do wonderful work on their books. Here are some memorable examples from both of us for when everything went right.

> *Alice:*
>
> *I worked on a memoir that brought estranged family members together for the first time after several years of pain and silence. That was a beautiful result from a book I wrote! I've become so close with that family that I'm now invited to birthday parties and baby showers.*
>
> *One of my dear clients was 78 when she decided to write her memoir, because she wanted people of her generation to know it's never too late for therapy and that we don't have to take our secrets to the grave. She has done multiple book tours and TV interviews and regularly meets with people who confide in her about their deepest secrets and regrets. She's able to be a blessing to many because she shared her story of healing.*

Alee:

I worked on a memoir with a client who was processing the abuse she endured in her childhood. She healed so much through the writing of the book that she felt confident enough to begin working toward change on the federal level. She now regularly attends congressional hearings, advocating for the elimination of the statute of limitations on reporting sexual crimes.

One of my favorite projects was a legacy book I created with a client who was grieving the traumatic loss of his partner. The writing journey was a gift to him, as it allowed him to memorialize his late husband in the pages of a book. It was an honor to work through a process that brought his late husband

to life on the page and, in essence, made him immortal.

TAKE ACTION

Potential Red Flag Phrases to Recognize

When we look back on red flag clients, they rarely hid their true colors for long and often displayed warning signs from the very first conversation. Here are some seemingly innocent phrases that should prompt you to ask follow-up questions before agreeing to work with them. Always dig deeper and ask clarifying questions like, "What does excellence look like for you?" or "Can you be more specific about why you thought the last writer you worked with sucked?"

Here are some key phrases to pay attention to:

- I am a very blunt person.

- My finances are tough right now because…

- I'm impatient.

- I'm very Type A.

- This book will make me millions.

- This is going to be really good for your career, so let's negotiate a lower rate.

- Let's just get started, and we can work out the payment details later.

- I'm not sure what I want, but I'll know it when I see it.

TAKE ACTION

Preset Your Boundaries

This chapter may have been dedicated to boundaries, but their importance is infused throughout every aspect of your business. Take the time to be intentional with them, and it will only benefit you in the long run. Reflect on boundaries you'd like to set for yourself and your business in the various categories below.

Communication	*Time*
Relationships	*Conversation*
Physical	*Financial*
Other	

CHAPTER 21

Coming Back from Failure

You will inevitably mess up boundaries, ignore red flags, and receive negative feedback at some point. Ultimately, you will fail, but failures bring equal opportunities like no other. Failure is indiscriminate and far-reaching. It's also not forever.

We have both been ineffective on projects and failed. Likewise, our colleagues have had to navigate disasters they created or unwittingly signed up for. Sometimes, our clients have come up short. Sometimes we've dropped the ball. But we all come back from it a little wiser, a little stronger, and with a little more resilience. (Dark humor helps. And did we mention ice cream?)

Alice: Fail Edition

Oh, the times I've messed up in my career. It's not constant, of course, but it happens. Over several decades and a ton of books, shit is going to happen. I'll share a funny story and a painful story so you can see the range.

When I was still working at the publishing house's book division, I didn't proofread a book spine when the designer sent it through email. This mistake will be forever burned into my brain. It was

---

a tiny gift book for Father's Day, and the word "fishing" was in the title. It was correct on the front cover, but the designer added an extra "i" in "fishing" on the spine, so it read, "Fishiing."

We printed and distributed 10,000 copies before someone caught it, and my boss came to me and said, "Have you seen this?"

Nope, sure hadn't. Clearly.

We had to recall 10,000 copies of a book because I didn't proofread the spine. Fail. I thought I might die. Or get fired. But I didn't.

Now for the pain.

I was helping someone write a science-heavy book about religion that had about thirty chapters, each containing multiple citations. Every time the client wanted to make an edit to a chapter, he'd resend it by email, but he didn't change the name of the file. This shouldn't have been an issue, because I could have simply resaved each chapter with a new name (something akin to Chapter11finalV3editedagainpart2pleasehelpmegod), but I missed a few of the attachments. Totally my fault.

This resulted in me not including several of the final-final-okay-this-time-it-is-final chapters in the full first draft. Oops.

My client was livid. He called to yell at me, questioning my abilities and my experience. Even though I had corrected the full manuscript by the very next morning, it was no use. I was fired. And I felt like an absolute toad for the errors.

Demoralization is real. And you know what? I survived. Demoralization can also incite resilience. And better record-keeping and versioning systems.

Alee: Fail Edition

Let's talk about failure. I've misfired many times. I've made errors, and I've also had moments of perceived failure because I didn't trust myself. It's always tough.

Once, I accidentally cc'd a random person on a client email when sharing her edited manuscript. Although most people generally couldn't care less about an idea that's not their own, clients are often worried others will steal their ideas. I didn't even realize the other, totally unrelated person was copied on it until the client responded, "Who is this other person? Is she an author?"

Talk about an oh-shit moment. It was a mess.

Another time, I took on a project where the author wanted to weave mindfulness into his book. During our initial interview, I said, "Mindfulness is a part of my being." I didn't realize until I started writing the book that I knew absolutely nothing about mindfulness beyond my guided meditations, which told me to "Stay in the present moment." I came to find out, that's not much. I sold myself as a seasoned practitioner of mindfulness, and I was 100% not. I soon found myself in a web of miscommunication and confusion. While it didn't cause the project to end, it made the work insanely difficult. Struggling with imposter syndrome is hard enough when you know what you're doing, let alone when you are an accidental real-life imposter.

Needless to say, I no longer make wild claims about my meditative skills.

MINI-FAILS ALONG THE WAY

- We've gotten our wires crossed and mentioned a detail from one author's backstory to another author.

- Alice once called an author by the wrong name . . . and even wrote the wrong name in the manuscript. (To be fair, he really did *not* look like he should have been named Paul.)

- Alee mistakenly did not record a vital client interview and had to ask the client for a redo of an extremely emotional conversation.

- We've had issues with version control and lost edits.

- We've missed deadlines and had to rework timelines.

Mistakes and negative feedback don't define you as a writer; how you respond to those situations does. Embrace the opportunity for growth, learn from the experience, and use it to fuel your determination to become a more resilient and confident writer. Remember, the road to success is paved with setbacks, but it's the journey of rising stronger that truly shapes your identity as a writer.

TAKE ACTION

Freelancer Affirmations

It's well-established that we'll all fail at some point, but it's important to differentiate between failing and being a failure. Stay true to yourself, and keep getting back up. On the days it feels too hard to do, repeat the following to yourself:

- Just because I made a mistake doesn't mean I have chosen this career by mistake.

- I am a worthwhile writer, even if someone doesn't like my words.

- I can and will work through any problem.

- Today, I will write the best I can, and that is enough.

- Tacos and tequila make everything better.

- Every setback is a setup for a comeback.

- I am constantly learning and growing in my craft.

- It's okay to take breaks and recharge; I'll come back stronger.

- I trust my voice and the stories I have to tell.

- My worth as a writer is not defined by a single piece of feedback.

If all else fails, take a nap, go to the movies, or call your best friend/mom/brother for a pep talk. Tomorrow is a new day, and we can guarantee that you'll be able to look back at your failure without wanting the floor to swallow you whole.

CHAPTER 22

Self-Care: Prioritizing Yourself and Making Time for Personal Projects

The world of writing and publishing is filled with creatives, and that skill set often comes with challenges like anxiety and depression. We've both dealt with these issues, and we've both done what was needed to work through them; making self-care a priority, taking some time off, and reminding ourselves that we're damn good at what we do.

MENTAL HEALTH AND SELF-CARE

Burnout is real. Alice experiences it about twice a year when her project load is heavier or deadlines are drawing near. When that happens, she journals more, books a trip, gets a massage, plays in her yard, and prioritizes lots and lots of naps. Most of the time, that's enough to get her out of a funk. She's also gotten really great at making stained glass pieces and loves that creative outlet.

Sometimes we get down because of life's circumstances, and sometimes it's because a project hits a bump or a roadblock. We can both recall clients who had completely disproportionate responses when an error couldn't be fixed or a timeline couldn't be moved. Learning how to deal with a client's explosive reaction in those moments is vital. It's often a trauma response. Figuring out how you're going to manage those situations before they happen can save you a lot of self-chastising and negative self-talk.

There have been many times when we looked back at those situations a day, a week, or even a month later, and realized, "Their response really had nothing to do with me." But at the time, we believed it had everything to do with us.

This is why it's so important to have several outlets for creativity, play, healing, and rest.

Alee: My Struggles with Mental Health

I've previously mentioned my bipolar disorder and CPTSD diagnoses. I have to admit, a lot of things are triggered when I'm working. The triggers don't necessarily come from the trauma stories; they actually come from my own thoughts. What if this client doesn't like me? What if they think I'm a bad writer? What if I can't actually do this?

This is why having a really strong mental health support system is so important. For me, that means having a psychiatrist and a therapist. I need someone I can just blurt things out to, because I'm under an NDA on every project I do, so I have to be cognizant of that fact. When I talk to a colleague, I have to speak very vaguely. While those conversations are helpful, it's nice to have someone who is subject to the same strict confidentiality policies I am, so I can be more open.

My therapist doesn't let me leave until we talk about work and what might be triggering me. The work feels really heavy sometimes. It helps to be able to put the stress down somewhere safe for a time.

WRITING FOR YOURSELF

Many of us got into this industry because we love to write. We often have our own writing projects going on in the background, which can be tough to prioritize. Since we spend so much of our time writing for other people, we've found it helpful to use the same process on ourselves. Alee treats her personal writing like one of her ghostwriting projects. She adds it to her to-do list and tackles it as if it's just another chapter in a client's book she's working on.

Alice keeps a huge running list of ideas for chapter titles, chapter topics, and book topics, because, when she's brainstorming titles for clients, phrases pop into her head that she could use on current or future projects. She also likes to keep tabs on ridiculous and funny stories in case she ever needs to reach back into the vault for something.

FIND YOUR SELF-CARE SWEET SPOT

Alee works 30-40-hour weeks. Alice used to work up to 60, depending on her project load, but now works more like 20-30 hours a week.

We both carry large client loads and are competitive with ourselves. Some ghostwriters do one book a year. Some (like us) write multiple books each year. Some keep their writing as a side hustle. Each of these paths is great. Your business is your business, just as much as your self-care is your self-care.

Self-care is an amalgam of finding your sweet spot and learning what you can handle. It includes setting boundaries with clients and with your business. Self-care is owning your "Hell, yes!" your "Hard pass," and your "I don't really want to, but I'll do it for now, because I have to pay my bills, and I'm building my career and growing my business."

Self-care is evolving, evaluating, and responding to your needs the way you respond to everyone else's. Sometimes it's a massage, sometimes it's hiking the Appalachian Trail or a round of golf. Sometimes it's five minutes alone, sometimes it's a bottle of wine with friends.

Know thyself, Writer. You'll figure it out.

TAKE ACTION

My Self-Care Plan

As a freelance writer, if you aren't taking care of yourself, you won't be able to take care of business. What does self-care mean to you, and how will you commit to yourself?

MY WEEKLY SELF-CARE PLAN

NAME: _____

THIS WEEK I'M GRATEFUL FOR

☐ _____

☐ _____

☐ _____

THIS WEEK'S TOP 5 SELF-CARE GOALS

☐ _____

☐ _____

☐ _____

SELF-CARE COMMITMENTS

I value	So I need	& I will honor this by
MENTAL		
EMOTIONAL		
PHYSICAL		
RELATIONSHIPS		
WORK		

CHAPTER 23

You've Got This, Writer

We would bet a million dollars that every ghostwriter out there had a few (okay, maybe more than a few) fleeting doubts before they dove headfirst into their first freelance writing project.

"What if I'm not good enough?"

"What if the client hates me?"

"What if I never get another project and have to find another line of work?"

"What if I have to sell foot pictures to pay my bills?" (Ahem, Alice . . .)

These are all valid concerns, but as you'll see as long as you stick with writing and continue to hone your craft, there's always a way forward. And your journey doesn't have to look like anyone else's for you to consider it successful.

Truth be told, we both had doubts and fears before getting started. Alice worried that she wasn't a good enough writer to write for others, that she'd forget how to spell, or that her talent would dim over time. Instead, her writing, confidence, and processes have improved with each project.

When presented with the idea of becoming a ghostwriter, Alee initially thought, *If I'm going to write a book, it's going to be for me*. She assumed that if she had this skill set, it should be treated with reverence—that she should be cautious about using it for others, as if her creative energy was finite. She worried that by helping others tell their stories, she'd be wasting something that was meant to be hers and hers alone. Now, she uses those skills to bring her clients' stories to life, and the creative process actually inspires her to continue writing her own content on the side.

The funny thing is, what we've discovered along the way is that these doubts and fears, while common, are false. When tackling our very first projects, we quickly realized that using our natural talents in a professional setting was one of the most freeing things we could do. Many years later, we still sometimes feel nervous when we begin a new project, but that just means we actually care about the client and the results!

Instead of struggling to make things work, pumping out spreadsheets, and working toward the goals of huge companies, we built lives where we could weave beautiful stories out of our clients' most intimate moments. We are no longer forcing ourselves to work; instead, we look forward to it, because we make the rules and we reap the rewards. That's the best part of working in your passion.

Over time, the work has not only been fulfilling; it's also been more financially gratifying than we ever imagined. As we've learned to value our talents and see ourselves as major assets to the people we work with, we've learned to charge what we deserve for the works of art we produce. This has allowed us to live lives that most people dream of, earning money by leveraging our natural skills.

Our hope for you, Dear Writer, is that you keep this book with you as you take a leap that will change your life in the most profound ways. Crack the spine, fold the pages, take a pen and highlighter to the text—wreck it, make it your own, even as you weave priceless stories for others.

Use this guide as a foundation for building the career you want. We're with you all the way.

Resources

LITERARY ORGANIZATIONS

Association of Ghostwriters:
https://associationofghostwriters.org/

Editorial Freelancers Association:
https://www.the-efa.org/

Nonfiction Author's Association:
https://nonfictionauthorsassociation.com/

National Association of Memoir Writers:
https://www.namw.org/

The Author's Guild:
https://authorsguild.org/

STYLE GUIDES

The Chicago Manual of Style (CMS):
https://www.chicagomanualofstyle.org/tools_citationguide.html

American Psychological Association Style and Grammar Guidelines:
(APA): https://apastyle.apa.org/style-grammar-guidelines

Modern Language of America (MLA):
https://style.mla.org/

Robert Hudson (editor), The Christian Writer's Manual of Style, Updated and Expanded Edition, April 11, 2004, Zondervan.

OTHER ONLINE RESOURCES

Jane Friedman "Reporting on the Publishing Industry": https://janefriedman.com/

Grammar Girl "Quick and Dirty Tips": https://www.quickanddirtytips.com/grammar-girl/

Publishers Marketplace (requires a subscription): https://www.publishersmarketplace.com/

Query Tracker "Helping Authors Find Literary Agents": https://querytracker.net/

About the Authors

Alice Sullivan is a #1 bestselling *Wall Street Journal* ghostwriter, *New York Times* bestselling editor (11 times over), collaborator, and speaker. An avid storyteller, she has written 66 books and edited over 1,300 titles since 2001. Several have hit bestseller status or received awards, including the 2024 International Impact Book Award for Health.

Her clients include speakers, educators, entrepreneurs, athletes, CEOs, and creatives. She specializes in memoir, business and thought leadership, and self-help/personal growth because she loves stories of triumph, determination, and personal reflection. Connect with her at alicesullivan.com.

Alee Anderson is a *Publishers Weekly* bestselling ghostwriter and a *New York Times* bestselling editor. She specializes exclusively in memoir and personal development books for trauma survivors, having supported the healing and recovery journeys of nearly 100 clients since 2015. Her clients include survivors of violent crimes, mass casualty events, abuse, chronic illness, and near-fatal accidents, as well as those processing the death of loved ones, recovering from attacks by serial perpetrators, and those living with CPTSD.

Alee believes deeply in the transformative power of storytelling and strives to make the world a better place with every word she writes. Learn more at aleeandersoneditorial.com.